Arabian
Delights

A Capital Lifestyles Book—Other books in the series include:

The Asian Diet: Get Slim and Stay Slim the Asian Way
by Diana My Tran

*The Family Table: Where Great Food, Friends and
Family Gather Together*
by Christy Rost

*The Kitchen Answer Book: Answers to All of Your Kitchen
and Cooking Questions*
by Hank Rubin

Kitchen Memories: A Legacy of Family Recipes from Around the World
by Anne Parsons and Alexandra Greeley

Nosthimia! The Greek American Family Cookbook
by Georgia Sarianides

Sabroso! The Spanish-American Family Cookbook
by Noemi Christina Taylor

*Savvy Eating for the Whole Family: Whole Foods, Whole Family,
Whole Life*
by Margaret McCullers Kocsis, MD

Tea & Etiquette: Taking Tea for Business and Pleasure
by Dorothea Johnson

Upper Crusts: Fabulous Ways to Use Bread
by Sheilah Kaufman

Save 25% when you order any of these and other fine Capital
titles from our website: www.capital-books.com.

Arabian Delights

Recipes & Princely Entertaining Ideas from the Arabian Peninsula

Amy Riolo

CAPITAL LIFESTYLES BOOK

CAPITAL
BOOKS, INC.
Sterling, Virginia

Capital Books, Inc.
P.O. Box 605
Herndon, Virginia 20172-0605

All photographs by Amy Riolo

ISBN 13: 978-1-933102-55-9

Library of Congress Cataloging-in-Publication Data

Riolo, Amy.
  Arabian delights : menus, recipes, & princely entertaining ideas
from the Arabian Peninsula / Amy Riolo. — 1st ed.
      p. cm. — (Capital series)
  Includes bibliographical references and index.
  ISBN 978-1-933102-55-9 (alk. paper)
  1. Cookery, Arab. 2. Cookery—Arabian Peninsula. 3.Entertaining.
4. Menus. I. Title. II. Series.
  TX725.A7R56 2007
  641.5953—dc22

                                              2007035047

Printed in the United States of America on acid-free paper that meets the American National Standards Institute Z39-48 Standard.

First Edition

10 9 8 7 6 5 4 3 2 1

To Maher, for supporting all of my decisions and sampling all of my recipes.

Contents

PART 2: SPECIAL CEREMONIES

PART 3: SIMPLER DELIGHTS

Foreword

People come together to experience the ambiance of a setting, camaraderie of friends, and, of course, food. Good food and good companionship are the main reasons most of us entertain. But I, like my many other "foodie" friends, am always looking for new ideas for entertaining and new cuisines to serve. *Arabian Delights* fits the bill! I was spellbound by the stories of Aladdin and Sherherazad and the magic of Arabia, a place of wonder and fantasy. Now all the wonder and delights of both old and new Arabia can be found in one book and can be duplicated in your own home for your family and friends. Amy Riolo offers suggestions for palatial feasts, special ceremonial foods, and simple delights in this wonderful, distinctive cookbook.

This exceptional new book allows us to broaden our culinary horizons by introducing the exciting and unfamiliar in food and hospitality. The recipes are simple but elegant, will enhance any family meal or festive occasion, and will inspire us to entertain in new, delightful ways. Amy uses her knowledge of Arabian culture, lore, and food to inspire us to go beyond our present culinary boundaries.

Amy brings her knowledge of international versatility to this collection of Arabian recipes. The recipes come from a multitude of places, from the kitchens of the royal palaces at Mina, Jeddah, Mecca, and Medina to the homes of extraordinarily hospitable people and vivacious street vendors.

The historic and cultural information is fascinating and guaranteed to please even those who simply like to read and never actually cook!

My love for food and culinary history and my thirst for knowledge led to my attending Amy Riolo's lecture at the Egyptian embassy titled "How the Three Religions of the World Shaped the Cuisine of Egypt." The lecture was fascinating. I could not wait to speak to Ms. Riolo when she was finished and discuss all the questions the lecture evoked for me. We talked for a while, and then I invited her to lunch so I could get to know her better. This was the beginning of a beautiful friendship. I found a kindred soul and expanded my knowledge of cooking and food history to include Middle Eastern, Italian, Moroccan, and Arabian cuisine.

Amy is a lovely, fascinating woman who speaks five languages, is an expert cook, and loves to share what she knows and what she does. Her book is unlike any other on the market.

Sheilah Kaufman
author, cooking teacher, food editor, and lecturer

Acknowledgments

I would like to express gratitude to my creator for enabling this book to be a part of my destiny. This book would not have been possible without the help of Sheilah Kaufman, an excellent friend, author, editor, cooking instructor, and mentor. I thank my wonderful friend, the talented Roman artist Liana Mari for the beautiful work that she contributed to this book. I would like to thank Kathleen Hughes and Amy Fries at Capital Books for their wonderful ideas and for the opportunity they have given me. I also truly appreciate the editorial guidance of Julie Kimmel. I also extend gratitude to my husband, Maher El Tanbedawy, for his willingness to taste new recipes, and to my sister-in-law, Soad El Tanbedawy, for sharing her knowledge of Arabian cuisine and culture with me. I would also like to thank His Majesty King Abdullah for the unparalleled hospitality extended to us during our stay at his guest palaces, as well as my Nonna, Angela Foti; my parents, Faith and Rick Riolo; and Yia Yia Mary Riolo for fueling my passion for good food at an early age. In addition, I also thank Dr. Norton Fishman, Kathleen Ammalee Rogers, Dr. Beth Tedesco, and Dr. Mary Lee Esty for enabling me to achieve my goals. Thank you to Raymond LaSala of the Mycological Association of Washington, D.C., for introducing me to Arabic desert truffles.

In Saudi Arabia, I would like to thank Dr. Omar Alsabti and Dr. Abdel Rahman for their excellent guidance, hospitality, and willingness to explain the history, traditions, and rituals of the Arabian culture. I would also like to thank our friends Emad Kshy and Batoul Alhalis, as well as Captain and Mrs. Zahri, for their hospitality in Saudi Arabia and eagerness to share cultural information, recipe ideas, and wonderful meals. And I would like to thank the numerous chefs and staff at the Mecca Guest Palace, Jeddah Conference Palace, Mina Guest Palace, and Medina Hilton for their tips, suggestions, and generosity.

Thank you to Dr. Abdullah Khouj at the Islamic Center of Washington, D.C., for arranging my *hajj* trip and for all of the guidance and knowledge he has shared with me and with many others over the years. And thank you to Muhieldin Awad Salih for organizing the trip for us. I would also like to thank the staffs at the Embassy of the Kingdom of Saudi Arabia, the Embassy of the Sultanate of Oman, and the Embassy of the Kingdom of Bahrain, and the Embassy of Kuwait for their willingness to help me with this project. I would also like to thank Barry Kaufman for his advice and for recipe tasting. I truly appreciate all of your contributions.

Introduction

The cuisine of the Arabian Peninsula combines healthful ingredients and time-honored techniques with exotic herbs, flowers, spices, and sometimes even incense. I came to know the exquisite cuisine of this region when I traveled to Saudi Arabia to participate in the annual pilgrimage to Mecca (spelled Makkah in Saudi Arabia*). I was with an American delegation that was sent to Saudi Arabia as part of the Royal Protocol. Our group stayed in the guest palaces in Mecca, Mina, and Jeddah. We were also able to see the splendors of the city of Medina.

The Great Mosque, also known as Masjid al Haram *in Arabic, in Mecca.*

---

*   I have chosen to use the American spellings for place names used in this book, such as Mecca and Medina, for ease of recognition.

Prior to traveling to Saudi Arabia, I had no idea what distinguished the cuisine of the Arabian Peninsula from that of other Arabic-speaking countries. After the first few meals, however, the regional differences in the cuisines became obvious. During my stay in Saudi Arabia, I had the opportunity to eat in the homes of friends in Jeddah and Mecca, and I was invited to the homes of many other locals on numerous occasions. These experiences taught me that hospitality and generosity are the key ingredients in all Arabian meals.

Modern Arabians enjoy serving food in large quantities to honor guests, just as their ancestors did. They make sure to provide their guests with as many options as possible, often serving numerous types of rice, meat, fish, and salad at the same meal. Arabians also take the flavor of food seriously. Dishes are tasted numerous times throughout the stages of preparation to ensure that they have been seasoned properly.

After being entertained with such lavishness, I began to reevaluate my own entertaining process. I wanted to create a way for myself, and other Americans, to entertain the Arabian way with minimal time and effort. In *Arabian Delights*, I have combined the authentic, easy-to-prepare recipes I've procured from friends and chefs with recipes adapted to suit the American lifestyle.

Many traditional Arabian recipes, like spit-roasted stuffed lamb, for example, are not practical enough to re-create in most homes. Communal meals designed to feed hundreds of people are similarly impractical for most Americans. Many modern Arabians rely upon domestic help, chefs, and carry-out food to create massive feasts. I've adjusted the menus used in this book so that Americans can fit them into their lifestyles. The recipes found in *Arabian Delights*, although Arabian in style, substance, and spirit, contain practical modern preparation techniques, and step-by-step instructions for cooks of all levels.

Once I selected the recipes to include in this book, I realized that the reader would like to know which items are appropriate for which occasions. For this reason, the book is divided into three parts: Palatial Feasts, Special Ceremonies, and Simpler Delights. Each chapter provides menus, recipes, and entertaining ideas to ensure that each event can be re-created with style and ease, or they can be used to celebrate your own holidays, special occasions, or simple meals. No menu needs to be followed to the letter. You may find it more practical at first to prepare only one or two items from a menu and eventually work up to the full menu. Keep in mind that there are no hard rules when entertaining Arabian style. Through mixing and matching items from various menus, you will create your own new traditions.

Your meal's mission is to please both yourself and your guests. I hope that you enjoy these menus, recipes, and entertaining ideas as much as I do. May they inspire you to create new and exciting ways of entertaining. May each morsel of food fill your heart with light and inspiration.

A History of Arabian Cuisine

As used in this book, the term "Arabian cuisine" includes the cuisine of Bahrain, Kuwait, Qatar, Oman, Saudi Arabia, the United Arab Emirates, and Yemen. The kitchens of these countries blend spice-infused aromas, intriguing visual presentations, fragrant flavors, and velvety textures with the sizzling sound of embers being lit to burn heavenly incense. Today's Arabian cuisine is one of the most healthful, diverse, and unique in the world. Its history is as captivating and distinct as its flavor and can be divided into three periods: antiquity, the seventh century and the advent of Islam, and modernity.

Evidence of crops on the Arabian Peninsula dates back five thousand years to when lush oases were the area's agricultural centers. The first known center is located in modern-day Yemen. The Hadhramaut region is located in southern Yemen and spans to the border of Oman in the east and Saudi Arabia in the north. In this region, the population is centered around towns built near water sources in the valleys. Many ancient aqueducts still provide seasonal water courses to crops in these areas today. Nomadic desert tribes traded for staples such as rice, dates, mutton, and lamb, which were indigenous to the Arabian Peninsula.

People living along the shores of the Red and Arabian Seas developed a love affair with seafood, which is as strong today as it was in ancient times. In antiquity, a large percentage of Arabians were fishermen. Lobster, crab, shrimp, tuna, grouper, king fish, shark, and other kinds of seafood are enjoyed throughout the region. People living along the coast traditionally offered their guests many kinds of fish and rice at one meal.

Inhabitants of the Arabian Peninsula traded with India, Africa, Central Asia, and the Levantine for thousands of years. In addition to providing area residents wealth, the years of trade spread cultural ideas, knowledge, and recipes throughout the region. Trade, and the ensuing addition of spices from faraway

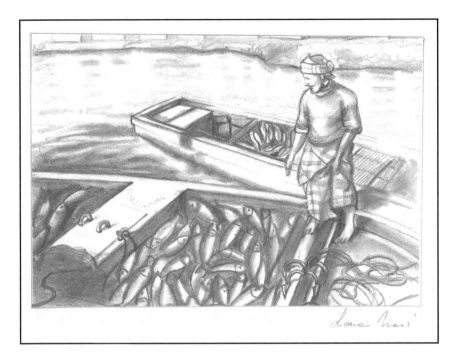

lands, elevated Arabian cuisine from its humble Bedouin origins to a new elegant status. As more spices became available, each country developed its own unique spice blends and recipes. From one basic spice mix came dozens of others. Today each mix is used with a specific type of food, whether fish, poultry, beef, lamb, or vegetables. Each spice vendor and cook has his or her own special blend for each food type.

Islam came to Arabia in the early seventh century, when the Prophet Muhammad* received the first verses of the *Qur'an* from the Angel Gabriel in a cave on top of Mount Hira (known as the Mountain of Light, "*Jabal al Noor,*" in Arabic) in Mecca, Arabia. The Prophet's wife and companions were the first people to adopt the new religion. By the time the Prophet died in 632,

---

* Although it is not written in the text of this book, in accordance with Islamic tradition, it is understood that the phrase "may peace be upon him" is uttered after Prophet Muhammad or other prophets are mentioned.

Islam had spread throughout Arabia. After his death, it continued to spread through the Arab world, Asia, North Africa, Sicily, and Spain.

There are five pillars of Islam:

1. *Shahada*, meaning the declaration that there is only one God and that the Prophet Muhammad is his last and final messenger.
2. *Salat*, meaning prayer and referring to the five prayers required of Muslims at specific times each day.
3. *Sawm*, or fasting, meaning that all adult Muslims who are physically able must abstain from food and drink (as well as other regulations) during the holy month of Ramadan.
4. *Zakat*, meaning charity, mandates that all Muslims who are financially able must donate a portion of their earnings to charity.
5. *Hajj,* the annual pilgrimage to Mecca, which must be completed once in a lifetime by Muslims who are physically and financially able to do so.

The practice of the five pillars changed daily life not only in Arabia, but all over the Islamic empire. The Arabian Muslims spread their culinary traditions to all of the lands they conquered. Pork and alcohol are prohibited in Islam, so these items were not part of the cuisine. *Halal* meat, which is slaughtered in accordance with Islamic guidelines to avoid waste and to minimize an animal's suffering, is the only meat a Muslim can eat. Halal meat regulations, like Kosher regulations, dictate that an animal can be slaughtered only in the name of God. The blood of the animal must be completely drained before its flesh can be consumed.

Trade continued to boom throughout the Islamic empire in the seventh century. Arab ships sailed to China for silk and porcelain, to the East Indies for spices, and to East Africa for gold. The goods were then sold to countries throughout the Mediterranean. During the Middle Ages, Arabian goods were coveted throughout Europe. Prices for the imported goods were so high that often only royalty could afford them on a regular basis. Commoners had to make due with small amounts only during the holidays. For this reason, many Christmas specialties throughout Europe contain Arabian spices and dried fruits.

Islam affected Arabian cuisine directly through the *hajj*. Over the years, many of the Muslims who traveled to Saudi Arabia during the *hajj* stayed there, and their cuisine became integrated into local cuisine.

Other aspects of Arabian cuisine that are rooted in religious tradition are standardized meal times and the practice of natural and spiritual medicine. After Islam was introduced, meals became centered around prayer times. Since five obligatory prayers are said at specific times each day, meals were timed to fit in between them. The five prayers are

1. *Fajr* (dawn prayer)
2. *Zohr* (noon prayer)
3. *Asr* (mid-afternoon prayer)
4. *Maghrib* (sunset prayer)
5. *Isha* (evening prayer)

Breakfast is always eaten after the dawn prayer, except during Ramadan, when Muslims fast between the dawn and sunset prayers. Lunch is always eaten after the noon prayer, and dinner is usually eaten after the evening prayer. Throughout the Arabian Peninsula, even today, all sense of time is centered around the five prayers. Friends agree to meet each other "after asr" and business meetings may take place "after zohr." This tradition was developed in the seventh century to help remind people of prayer times and therefore to encourage worship. Large numbers of people eating and praying at the same times also promotes a sense of community and lends a unique rhythm to life.

The medical and nutritional advice given by the Prophet Muhammad has been studied by Islamic *hakims* (physicians), who in turn created a new regime of natural medicine for Muslims. Islamic medicine created guidelines for eating and drinking based upon the body's elements. Certain foods, such as honey, dates, water, the nigella (known as the "blessed seed"), and fenugreek, were found to be useful for treating a wide variety of ailments.

The Prophet promoted eating and drinking while sitting upright to aid digestion. He also forbade people to eat while lying on their stomachs and discouraged reclining while eating because it obstructed the digestive tract. Other practices included avoiding mixing multiple hot foods together in the same meal; instead, the Prophet promoted eating one hot and one cold dish together. He also recommended that dinner should never be skipped and reminded followers that eating even a few dates is better than eating nothing. The Prophet Muhammad also commented on the benefits of a wide range of herbs, spices, and foods, many of which have been scientifically proved to be true in modern times.

The Prophet also recommended many specific prayers, and supplications were prescribed as a spiritual treatment for illness. Even today many people recite these prayers and blow into water or food before eating it believing it will be more nutritious for the body. Others inscribe words or one of the ninety-nine names of God onto pieces of bread before eating it in order to receive special blessings.

Modern Arabian cuisine, like modern American cuisine, is considered by natives to be a melting pot of many different fares. Increased opportunity for wealth in the region has brought people from around the world to the Arabian Peninsula for work. Many of the immigrants work in and own restaurants. Their signature dishes have become part of today's Arabian cuisine.

Improved standard of living and

Homemade pita bread, rolls topped with the "Blessed Seed" and sesame seeds, and French bread topped with tomato sauce.

modern transportation have made it possible for people of the Arabian Peninsula to travel abroad and try different cuisines. When they return home, they are eager to incorporate the new foods they tasted into their traditional dishes. As a result, cities like Jeddah, Riyadh, Masqat, Dubai, and Doha are filled with international chain restaurants. American, European, Indian, and Middle Eastern restaurants are everywhere. A trip to the supermarket in any one of these cities reveals famous American and French brands offered side by side with traditional Arabian foods. Because so many international items are offered, they aren't placed in separate sections as they are in American supermarkets. Foreign foods are simply accepted as part of the Arabian culinary family.

Regional Differences in Arabian Cuisine

Each country and region of the Arabian Peninsula has its own basic traditional diet, which has grown and diversified over the years. Some dishes are available in all countries, and these dishes vary only with the spices used to season them. They include ingredients that were continually available to the Arabians throughout all phases of history and that are preferred in modernity. Some recipes are completely unique to specific countries or regions because their ingredients are not found everywhere and are indigenous to lands that had remained secluded for long periods. The remainder of the Arabian Peninsula's gastronomic delights are the result of the integration of popular foreign dishes into Arabian cuisine.

Bahrain

Bahrain is made up of thirty-three islands in the heart of the Arabian Gulf. It is located just more than fifteen miles east of Saudi Arabia and is known as the "Gateway to the Gulf." Once part of an ancient trade route connecting the East and West, it is now an international business center.

Pearls found in the Arabian Sea, dates, and produce grown in desert oases were traditionally Bahrain's main economic producers. Nomadic tribes on the islands used to live off seafood, wheat, and dates. The flavors of the traditional dishes were enhanced with spices obtained from the trade routes to modern-day Iraq, Iran, and India. Twentieth-century oil wealth enabled the citizens of Bahrain to enjoy the luxury of the international food scene along with their traditional cuisine. Bahrain is now home to many upscale restaurants, modern malls, and museums.

Kuwait

Kuwaiti cuisine is based upon its indigenous tribal traditions, the contributions of immigrants from the Arab world and

Southeast Asia, and imported items. Today Bedouin, Indian, Pakistani, Turkish, and Arabian dishes are all part of the local diet. The national dish of Kuwait is *Kouzi*, a spit-roasted lamb stuffed with chicken, rice, eggs, and other savory items. Kuwaitis also have their own spice mixes. Dates and various wheat products are consistent staples of the Kuwaiti diet. Kuwaiti dishes, taking their inspiration from the Indian subcontinent, have become part of the national cuisine. *Machbous* is a popular dish consisting of mutton, chicken, or fish served over fragrant rice. It is closely related to Indian *Biryani*.

Kuwaiti cooking methods have changed over the years, as has the people's diet. Prior to the eighteenth century, Kuwaiti cuisine was very basic. One-pot meals prepared over charcoals were consumed by the locals. By 1760 Kuwaiti ships and camel caravans traveled to Baghdad and Damascus to trade wares. There, the traders witnessed the cuisines of the Abbasid and Ayyubid empires, which had already recognized cooking as an art form. The traders brought back with them a new style of cooking in which rice, meats, and vegetables were cooked separately, and added together just before being served. By the nineteenth century, Kuwait became a bustling center of commerce. Its newly obtained spices were used to create elaborate spice mixes, which further enhanced the complexity of traditional recipes.

Qatar

Qatar has been inhabited for millennia. There, nomadic tribes once lived off rice, dates, and sheep products, as they did in other parts of the region. Coastline dwellers enjoyed fish and seafood. Red snapper, lobster, crab, shrimp, and king fish were all plentiful.

In the eighteenth century, most citizens made their living as fishermen

Grilled prawns over arugula

and pearl divers. By 1850 Qatar had become a pearl diving capital. Pearl divers' diets were centered on carbohydrates, which were necessary to maintain their high energy levels. By the 1930s the pearl market had collapsed, and Qatar's economy suffered a hard blow. By the end of the decade, however, oil was discovered, and the people of Qatar began enjoying a strong economic boost.

In 1783 Persians invaded Qatar and brought their own culinary traditions with them. The Ottoman Turks occupied the country beginning in 1872, and the English established a binding political treaty with Shiekh Al Thani once the Turks left, at the beginning of World War I. On September 1, 1971, Qatar declared its independence, but its modern cuisine remains a blend of its ancient traditions, foreign rule, and modern, international flavors.

Oman

The geography of modern-day Oman includes mountains and plains, desert and sea. Fish is a staple in the Omani diet and the second largest economic producer in the country. One quarter of Omani citizens earn their living as fishermen. Shark, king fish, tuna, grouper, snapper, sardines, anchovies, and cuttlefish are all caught off Oman's shores.

Spices are also very close to the hearts of the Omani people. Their local blend is called *bizaar*. *Lumi*, or dried limes, which are used in spice mixtures all over the Arabian Peninsula, come from Oman. The Omani obtained prized spices and rich recipes from the East African island of Zanzibar, which they ruled during the nineteenth century.

Frankincense is also plentiful in Oman, where the burning of incense is a veritable art form. Frankincense comes from a resinous gum on the Boswellia Sacra tree, which grows in southern Oman. Omani frankincense is exported all over the world and at one time was worth as much as gold. The gum resin is believed to open the seventh chakra of the body and therefore expand consciousness. It is often balanced by myrrh, which is known for its ability to calm a person.

According to Gina Hyams in *Incense: Rituals, Mystery, Lore*, Oman was once part of the ancient Incense Trail, which was a 2,400-mile-long route through Oman and Saudi Arabia to Jordan. The Incense Trail intersected the Silk Road, which opened up even further trade opportunities for the Omanis.

Saudi Arabia

In Saudi Arabia today, many dishes are based upon Indian, Indonesian, Pakistani, Turkish, Moroccan, Syrian, and Egyptian influences that were introduced by traders, pilgrims, and immigrants. Saudi Arabia is made up of three regions: the *Hijazi* (the western part of Saudi Arabia bordering the Red Sea), the *Najdi* (the central region highlands between the mountains of *Hijaz*), and the *Khaliji* (the eastern portion of the country bordering the Arabian Sea). Cuisine from other Arabian countries located to the east of Saudi Arabia is also collectively referred to in Arabic as *Khaliji* cuisine.

The original cuisine of the Hijazi region (encompassing the cities of Medina, Mecca, Al-Ta'if, and Jeddah) consisted of meat, vegetables, and wheat. The cuisine of Jeddah also included an enormous amount of seafood because it is located on the Red Sea. Although Medina, Mecca, and Al-Ta'if are not far away from Jeddah by modern standards, limited transportation options in antiquity made it difficult to transport fish to these areas.

The Najd, or central highland region of Saudi Arabia, remained relatively isolated from the rest of the country prior to the seventh century. Originally, dishes from this area were based on wheat, rice, milk, and dates. Crushed wheat also comes from this region. Traditionally the wheat was pounded by hand, but nowadays food processors are usually used.

After Islam was introduced to the Najd, many people became traders and often returned home from their travels with a variety of foods that greatly enhanced the local diet. For the Muslim *Eid al Adha* (Feast of the Sacrifice), Najdis prepare *Al Bideya*, a dish consisting of wheat cooked in lamb broth, topped with onions, covered with dough, topped with saffron, rose water–infused rice, and lamb. The dish is garnished with boiled eggs and vegetables. Each year on *Eid al Adha*, neighbors congregate to prepare and enjoy this unique dish together.

The eastern or Khaliji region of Saudi Arabia is known for its extensive use of spices and chilies, which were obtained from traders traveling via the Arabian Sea and Indian Ocean. Sea trading, fishing, and pearl diving are all part of this region's history, and seafood was always popular with the people of Khaliji. They serve grouper, mackerel, and snapper with various rice dishes, and travel inland to the oasis towns to obtain produce and staples like wheat, sugar, tea, and coffee. The Khalijis call rice "*aish*," which means life in the local dialect, and shows the importance of rice as a staple.

Today people from all Saudi regions enjoy one another's cuisines more often thanks to modern transportation, the computer, and an increased number of cookbooks. Chefs and home cooks create foods from all over the world, while still preserving Saudi traditions.

United Arab Emirates

The United Arab Emirates (UAE) was founded in 1971 and is located on the Persian Gulf and the Gulf of Oman. The majority of its population is foreign born and consists of large numbers of Pakistanis, Indians, Sri Lankans, and Filipinos. Abu Dhabi and Dubai are the largest cities in the UAE. Both cities are extremely modern and offer cosmopolitan, international cuisine.

The people of this region were seafarers prior to the arrival of Islam in the seventh century. They established successful trade ports and commercial centers. With the expanse of the oil industry in the 1960s, the economy and landscapes of the area changed drastically. Both the UAE's population and agricultural production have increased to ten times their original numbers in the past twenty-eight years. Nowadays the UAE is agriculturally self-sufficient and produces many crops, some of which are exported to Europe.

Renowned chefs come from all over the world to produce gourmet meals in five-star restaurants and resorts in Dubai. The local immigrant population has opened restaurants offering foods of their homelands. Eating in Dubai, one has the chance to explore cuisine from the whole world, just as someone eating in New York City does. Dubai even has its own food channel called Fatafeat, which means "crumbs." It broadcasts both English and Arabic cooking programs.

Yemen

Yemen is the most arable spot on the Arabian Peninsula. Native Yemenis trace their lineage back to the Prophet Noah. Yemen's population is mostly Muslim but includes a Jewish minority. Yemeni cuisine celebrates spices, chilies, and coffee. Coffee, wheat, and corn grow in the Arabian plateau where strong monsoon rains fall in the summer. Although coffee grew prior to the thirteenth century in Ethiopia and Yemen, it is believed to have been roasted for the first time in that century in Yemen. Yemen's port city of Mocha is the origin of the English word "mocha," which is used to describe coffee-flavored drinks and desserts.

Coffee culture spread through the Arabian Peninsula with the help of Imams, or Muslim clerics, who learned about its stimulant properties and used it as an aid to stay awake during long hours of devotion. Arabian coffee is a milder roast than espresso and American-style coffee. It is yellowish-gold in color and is served in eggshell-sized cups, similar to Japanese sake cups. Arabic coffee is always served unsweetened with dates as an accompaniment to balance out the flavors.

Most people mix the coffee with cardamom, using equal parts of each. A pinch of saffron may also be added on special occasions. Fancy gold, silver, and copper pots with long, curved spouts similar to a pelican's beak are used to prepare the coffee. Pieces of straw are tied together and stuffed into the spout to strain the cardamom pods while serving. Today, modern supermarkets sell premixed coffee and ground cardamom.

Tips to Remember
when entertaining with the menus
and recipes in this book

1. Make sure that you are comfortable with each of the recipes on the menu.
2. Read the recipes through a few times before making them.
3. Practice making dishes on other occasions before entertaining with them.
4. Identify which items (if any) you will need to mail order or purchase from a specialty grocer.
5. Make as many of the items in advance as possible.
6. Adjust each of the menus to reflect your budget, local availability and dietary restrictions of guests, if necessary.
7. Adjust the quantities of ingredients in the recipes to reflect the number of guests
8. The menus in this book are mere suggestions. Mix and match different recipes as you see fit to come up with your own Arabian meals.
9. Arabian meals are not meant to be "fussy." Although many of the menus contain quite a few dishes, they are meant to be prepared leisurely.
10. Enlist the help of family and friends to prepare more labor-intensive recipes and create an entertaining opportunity out of cooking together.

PART 1
PALATIAL FEASTS

Royal Wedding Reception

Eid Holiday Feast

Arabian Tea Party

Palace Spice Brunch

CHAPTER 1
Royal Wedding Reception

Fairy tale wedding receptions are commonplace across the Arabian Peninsula. Romantic decorations including shining lights, exotic ice sculptures, abundant flowers, beautifully set tables, and a traditional wedding cake decorate the reception area. Regional tradition dictates whether the bride may enter the room from a balcony trimmed in lights alone or with her husband. The couple enjoys the reception feast seated on a stage in gold-gilded chairs or on an elegant sofa.

Small plates of pastries, chocolates, and dates are used to garnish guest tables. Arabic coffee and a wide variety of juices are served. Prominent families' receptions include numerous buffet tables, for appetizers, soups, breads, salad, fruits, and desserts. Live music may be traditional, Western, or a combination of styles depending on the bride and groom's ethnic background.

The following menu is wonderful for a small wedding reception because it incorporates many flavorful and unique items that can be prepared ahead of time. The menu's themes are pairs and rings. Its incorporation of the "marriage" of different ingredients, romantic recipe names, the use of the traditional ring shape, and the color red make this menu a perfect choice for the celebration of not only a wedding, but an anniversary or engagement party as well.

Royal Wedding Menu

Spice Mix:
> Saudi Spice Mix (*Baharat*)

Appetizers:
> Mini Swiss Chard Omelets Topped with *Labna* (*Selek bi Labne*)
>
> Cheese and Blessed Seed Turnovers (*Sambusak bil*

Jebna wa Habit al Baraka)
  Sesame Chapati Bread (*Khubz Chabati bil Simsim*)
Soup:
  Meat Dumplings in Consommé (*Hasaa bil Shish barak*)
Salads:
  Eggplant, Tomato, and Chili Pepper Salad (*Salata
     Batinjan bil Tomatum wa Filfil*)
  Beet Salad with Tahini Dressing (*Salata bil Bangar wa
     Tahina*)
Main Courses:
  Yogurt and Spice Marinated Leg of Lamb (*Fakhz bil
     Laban*)
  Saudi Chicken and Date *Tajine* with Saffron Couscous
     (*Tajin Dajaj wa Tamr bil Couscous*)
  Red Rice and Shrimp Skillet (*Roz Ahmar bil Jamberi*)
  Beef *Makhtoum* (*Makhtoum*)
Drinks:
  Rose Cooler (*Assir Ward*)
  Golden Dream Cocktail (*Cocktail Halm min Dahab*)
Desserts:
  Wedding Cake (purchased)
  Sesame Ring Cookies (*Biskoweet bil Simsim*)
  Mahlab Ring Cookies (*Mahlabayat*)
Tabletop:
  Assorted Pastries and Chocolates (purchased)
Favor:
  Almond-Stuffed Chocolate-Covered Dates (*Tamr bil
     Lowz wa Chocolata*)

Saudi Spice Mix (*Baharat*)

This spice mix is indispensable for preparing the recipes in
this book. I like to prepare it in large quantities ahead of time.
That way, when I'm cooking I don't need to take the time to find
the individual spices. Feel free to alter this recipe to your tastes,
the way Arabian housewives do.

Ingredients:
1/4 cup ground black pepper

1/8 cup dried coriander, ground
1/8 cup ground cloves
2 tablespoons ground cumin
1/8 cup ground cardamom
1 teaspoon fresh nutmeg
1/4 cup paprika
1/8 cup ground ginger
2 dried limes*

Preparation:

Place the first 8 ingredients in a glass jar. Cover jar with lid
  and shake to combine.
Grind the dried limes in a coffee or spice grinder until they
  reach a powder consistency. Add to the spice mixture,
  cover, and shake to mix well.
Store for up to 2 months in a tightly sealed jar, in a cool,
  dark place.
Makes about 1 cup.

Mini Swiss Chard Omelets Topped with Labna (Selek bi Labne)

These delicious and healthful omelets can be made ahead of
time and frozen. If you prefer, spinach can be used instead of
Swiss chard. These omelets make an elegant appetizer when
placed on a silver or gold tray.

Ingredients:

1 cup *labna* (yogurt cheese)*
Salt, to taste
3 cups fresh Swiss chard
6 tablespoons vegetable, corn, or canola oil, divided
1 small onion, diced
5 large eggs

---

* See "Where to Buy Guide" for information.
** *Labna* can be found in Middle Eastern and Greek markets, as
     well as some gourmet grocers. For mail order sources, refer to the
     "Where to Buy Guide."

1/4 cup flour
1 teaspoon dried mint
1/4 cup parsley, chopped
1 teaspoon Saudi Spice Mix (see page 3)

Preparation:

Mix *labna* with salt in a small bowl. Refrigerate until needed.

Place Swiss chard in a medium saucepan, cover with water, and bring to a boil over high heat. Reduce heat to medium and cook until tender, 10 to 15 minutes. Drain well and set aside to cool. (This step can be completed a day ahead of time.)

Heat 2 tablespoons of oil in a small frying pan, and sauté onion until lightly golden. Remove from heat and set aside to let cool.

Combine eggs, flour, onion, mint, parsley, and Saudi Spice Mix.

Heat remaining oil in a large frying pan over medium heat. When oil is hot, drop tablespoons of batter into pan in a circular motion (as if shaping silver dollar-sized pancakes). When edges are cooked through (1 to 2 minutes), turn and cook the other side. Place on a large serving platter.

Put *labna* into a cake-decorating bag (or a plastic sandwich bag with one corner of the bottom snipped off). Squeeze a dollop of *labna* into the middle of each pancake, or just use a spoon to place the *labna* on the pancake. Serve immediately.

Serves 4 to 6.

Tip: *For a quick weeknight dinner, you can make 1 large omelet and cut it into single-size servings.*

Cheese and Blessed Seed Turnovers
(*Sambusak bil Jebna wa Habit al Baraka*)

These simple turnovers are a delicious addition to any party. The blessed seed is known as the nigella seed in the West. The Prophet Muhammad claimed that this seed could be used to cure everything except death. It is a popular addition to Middle Eastern breads, pickles, and pastries.

Ingredients:
1 pound feta cheese, drained well
Salt, to taste
Freshly ground pepper, to taste
1/4 cup fresh parsley, chopped
1 large egg
Flour, for dusting pastry
1 (1.1 pound) package puff pastry, at room temperature
1 large egg yolk, whisked
1/8 cup nigella seeds* or black poppy seeds

Preparation:
Preheat oven to 350°F.

Mix cheese, salt, pepper, parsley, and egg in a medium bowl
and set aside.

Dust a work surface with flour and roll out puff pastry into
2 large rectangles, about 2-inches longer and wider than
their original size. Cut dough into 4 equal strips lengthwise. Cut the strips into 3 1/2-inch squares. Place a
teaspoon of cheese mixture in the middle of each square.
Brush water around edges of squares and fold in half
to seal. Brush excess flour off pastry, and then brush tops
with egg yolk. Sprinkle nigella or poppy seeds on top.

Place on lined, thick baking sheets to prevent the bottoms from
burning. Bake 20 to 25 minutes until golden. Serve warm.

Serves 10 to 12.

*Tip: These turnovers can be made ahead of time, frozen, and
defrosted a few hours before eating.*

Sesame Chapati Bread
(Khubz Chabati bil Simsim)

Chapati is the delicious, tender, unleavened bread of Pakistan. A similar bread is prepared in India, where it is called
naan. Chapati was introduced to the Arabian Peninsula by
Pakistani immigrants who moved to the region after the economic boom in the late twentieth century. Now it is an integral

---

*   See "Where to Buy Guide" for purchasing information.

part of Arabian cuisine, just as it is in its native homeland.

I first experienced sesame chapati at the Jeddah Conference Palace in Saudi Arabia, where it was made in a hot clay oven, called a *tandoor*. One of the bakers at the palace would prepare chapati daily for the kitchen staff and servers, who were predominately from Pakistan and Bangladesh. Waiters brought baskets of the hot, tender bread studded with sesame seeds to each table. The bread became the highlight of our meals while we were in Jeddah. One day at lunch, we were served regular pita bread and European-style breads that were

View of the Red Sea from the Jeddah Conference Palace in Jeddah, Saudi Arabia.

commercially prepared. We asked for "the special bread" and were told it was available only at dinner. Dinnertime came and the bread was nowhere to be found. We once again inquired about it and were told it was the baker's day off. We wondered if the baker knew how much we were anticipating his return and that his bread had made such an enormous impression on us.

If you've never made bread before, don't hesitate to try this recipe. The soft and buttery dough is a real treat to work with!

Ingredients:
2 cups unbleached white bread flour
1/2 teaspoon salt
1 (0.6-ounce) package fresh yeast*

---

* Fresh yeast can usually be found near the butter in the dairy case at supermarkets.

5 tablespoons clarified butter (ghee), divided
1 large egg
1/2 cup sesame seeds

Preparation:
Sift flour and salt together in a large bowl.
In a small bowl, cream the yeast with 4 tablespoons lukewarm water and let rest for 15 minutes.
Add yeast mixture, 1/2 cup lukewarm water, 3 tablespoons
clarified butter, and egg to the flour and mix well to
combine. Continue mixing until a soft dough forms.
Turn dough out onto a lightly floured surface and knead for
10 minutes until smooth and elastic.
Place in a large bowl that has been lightly greased with clarified butter. Turn dough to coat, and cover with lightly
greased plastic wrap. Let rise in a warm, draft-free place
for 1 1/2 to 2 hours, or until doubled in bulk.
Preheat the broiler. Lightly grease a sheet of aluminum foil
large enough to cover the bottom of the broiler.
Turn the dough out onto a lightly floured surface and punch
down. Divide into four equal pieces and shape into balls.
(Dough may be frozen at this point.) Roll the dough out
into oval shapes approximately 7 inches long and 4
inches wide. Place two pieces of dough onto aluminum
foil. Brush more clarified butter on top of each oval and
sprinkle with sesame seeds. Broil for 2 to 3 minutes, or
until lightly golden and puffed up. Turn over, brush with
butter, and sprinkle with sesame seeds. Continue to
broil for another 1 to 2 minutes, or until golden. Repeat
with remaining two pieces of dough.
Serve warm or cool. Wrap in plastic and then aluminum foil
to freeze.
Serves 4.

*Tip: Although chapati is traditionally served fresh out of the
oven, it also freezes well. Try doubling this recipe and
freezing the extra half. Defrost the bread when needed, and
reheat under the broiler for 1 minute.
You can also freeze the dough, defrost it, and proceed with
the rest of the recipe another time.*

Meat Dumplings in Consommé
(Hasaa bil Shish barak)

Shish barak is the Arabian version of the Italian *Tortelloni in Brodo*. It's a uniquely satisfying soup that combines rich broth with plump, meat-filled dumplings. Most modern cooks in the Arabian Peninsula buy these dumplings pre-made. Making them by hand, however, is not difficult. A good ravioli cutter will enable you to cut the dough and seal the edges at the same time. Plus, preparing the dumplings yourself allows you to be creative with the fillings. Children enjoy filling the dumplings a great deal. When making dumplings from scratch, keep in mind that they need hours to dry. They may also be dried overnight in the refrigerator.

If you have no time to make the dumplings yourself, you can substitute a high-quality, ready-made meat tortelloni.

Ingredients:
For the filling:
2 tablespoons corn oil
1/2 pound ground beef or lamb, rinsed and drained well
1 small onion, grated and drained
2 tablespoons Saudi Spice Mix (see page 3)
1 teaspoon salt
For the dumplings:
3 1/2 cups unbleached, all-purpose flour, plus extra for rolling
1 cup whole milk
2 tablespoons vegetable oil
1/2 teaspoon salt
For the soup:
8 cups chicken or beef stock or Spice-Infused Stock (see page 31)
2 teaspoons tomato paste
Salt, to taste
Freshly ground pepper, to taste
1/4 cup fresh cilantro

Preparation:
To make the filling, heat oil in a large skillet over medium heat.
    Add meat, grated onion, Saudi Spice Mix, and salt. Stir
    well and cook until meat is brown. Take off heat to cool.
This step can be done a day in advance.

When it has cooled, drain excess oil from the meat using a colander. Refrigerate until needed.

Meanwhile, dust a cookie sheet with a handful of flour.

Mix all dumpling ingredients in food processor to form a ball. Use a spatula to remove dough from the food processor and place it on a work surface. Shape dough into 2 balls and set on the work surface at least 4 inches apart; cover with a kitchen cloth and let rest for 30 minutes.

After 30 minutes, roll out each dough ball into a rectangle approximately 12x12 inches and 1/4-inch thickness. Lightly dust the top of the dough, and cut into six 2-inch strips vertically. Working vertically, place 1/2 teaspoons of meat mixture 1 1/2 to 2 inches apart along the first strip. Do not fill the next strip. Continue filling every other strip, until half are topped with meat mixture and half are not.

With a rolling pin, lightly roll over the empty strips to make them slightly wider and longer than the strips topped with filling. Place the empty strips over the strips with filling. Use a ravioli cutter, or a sharp knife, to cut out the filled dumplings. If using a ravioli cutter, the edges of the dumplings will be sealed as you cut. If using a knife, press around perimeter of the squares with the edge of a fork to seal.

Cut one of the long edges into a half-moon shape by removing the corners. Wrap the long end of the rectangle around the tip of your pinkie finger, pressing pointed ends over each other to seal. Continue until all pieces are finished. Place on a cookie sheet dusted with flour.

Allow dumplings to dry out, turning every few hours, a minimum of two times per side until completely dry. (Alternatively, they can be left in the refrigerator to dry overnight).

Bring stock, tomato paste, salt, and freshly ground pepper to a rapid boil in a large stockpot. Add dumplings and cook until tender, about 6 to 8 minutes. Taste and adjust seasonings, if necessary.

Garnish with cilantro. Serve warm.

Serves 6 to 8. Makes about 50 dumplings.

Tip: You may also make the dumplings in advance, freeze them, and defrost and add them to boiling broth when needed. They also taste great when boiled in water, drained and cooled slightly, and dressed with good quality plain yogurt.

Eggplant, Tomato, and Chili Pepper Salad (Salata Batinjan bil Tomatum wa Filfil)

This is a hot and healthy salad that takes only minutes to prepare. It works well on buffets or as a simple side dish during a busy weeknight. When choosing eggplants, look for small ones with smooth, shiny skin and no bruises. Tomatoes should be bright red, firm, and kept outside of the refrigerator to yield the best flavors.

Ingredients:

2 1/2 cups canola oil, divided
4 small (4- to 5-inch-long) eggplants, sliced into
    1/4-inch-thick slices
4 roma tomatoes, sliced into 1/4-inch-thick slices
3 green chili peppers, seeded
1/4 cup distilled white vinegar
Salt, to taste
Freshly ground black pepper, to taste
Pinch of chili powder or paprika
Plain yogurt for garnish, if desired

Preparation:

Heat 2 cups canola oil in a large frying pan over medium heat. When oil is hot, carefully lower eggplant slices into pan. Do not crowd skillet. Fry eggplant 3 to 5 minutes per side until lightly golden and cooked through. Remove with a slotted spoon and place onto a platter lined with paper towels. Continue with remaining eggplant.

Fry roma tomatoes in the same manner and place onto a platter lined with paper towels.

Fry chili peppers in the same manner and place onto a platter lined with paper towels.

Whisk remaining 1/2 cup canola oil, vinegar, salt, pepper,

and chili powder or paprika together in a small bowl to form a dressing.

Place fried eggplant, tomato, and pepper slices onto a large serving platter. Top with dressing. Taste and adjust seasonings if necessary. Serve at room temperature.

Serves 4.

Beet Salad with Tahini Dressing (Salata bil Bangar wa Tahina)

Beets were once used as a dye in the Arabian Peninsula. The beet's beautiful ruby color makes it a perfect choice for a red-themed wedding reception. A beet's high iron content makes it a natural alternative to medical treatments for anemia.

In this recipe, beets are topped with delicious tahini (sesame paste). If making this recipe ahead of time, keep the dressing aside and drizzle it over the salad just before serving. Be aware that beets stain. Make sure to protect your countertops and clothing before handling them.

Ingredients:

1 pound (3 to 4) medium beets, leaves removed, scrubbed, and peeled
Salt, to taste
1 tablespoon distilled white vinegar
Juice of 1 lemon
1/4 cup tahini
1/2 cup plain yogurt, drained well

Preparation:

Place beets in a medium saucepan with salt and white vinegar. Cover with 5 cups water and bring to a boil over medium-high heat. Reduce heat to medium and continue cooking, uncovered, for 45 to 60 minutes, or until beets are tender.

In the meantime, mix lemon juice and tahini together in a small bowl. Taste and add salt if necessary.

When they are finished cooking, drain beets well and reserve liquid for making Red Rice with Shrimp (see page 16). Cut beets into 1/4-inch-thick slices. Spread yogurt onto the bottom of a serving platter. Arrange beet slices on top of the yogurt. Spoon sesame paste on top of the beets.

Serve warm or chilled.

Serves 4.

Yogurt and Spice Marinated Leg of Lamb (Fakhz bil Laban)

Marinating lamb in yogurt and garlic produces a succulent and tender piece of meat. Some Arabians marinate the meat in half of the marinade mixture and reserve the remaining half to slather on the cooked meat before it is served. Others serve the unused marinade as a sauce alongside the meat. I like to use all of the mixture as the marinade and forego the extra coating and sauce.

Serving lamb to guests is the ultimate demonstration of hospitality throughout the Arabian Peninsula. For both weddings and holidays, it is traditional to serve whole lambs that have been roasted in pits. I have used leg of lamb for this celebratory occasion because it is easier to find in America and to prepare in modern kitchens.

Ingredients:

1 (5- to 6-pound) leg of lamb, bone trimmed
10 garlic cloves, slivered
2 teaspoons Saudi Spice Mix (see page 3)
Salt, to taste
1 cup yogurt
2 tablespoons tomato paste
3 tablespoons mayonnaise
1/4 cup corn oil

Preparation:

Using a carving knife, make small slashes all over the leg of lamb and place it in a roasting pan. Stuff garlic slivers into the various slashes. Combine the spice mix, salt, yogurt, tomato paste, mayonnaise, and oil in a medium bowl. Spread the marinade over the lamb. Refrigerate, covered, for 2 hours or overnight.

Preheat oven to 350°F. Place lamb in oven, cover with

aluminum foil, and bake for 3 1/2 to 4 hours, until meat is tender and falling off of the bone.

Remove lamb from oven and let rest 10 minutes before carving. Serve warm.

Serves 8 to 10.

Tip: Use leftover lamb for sandwiches the next day, or add it to Fragrant Vermicelli Soup (see page 30).

Saudi Chicken and Date *Tajine* with Saffron Couscous (*Tajin Dajaj wa Tamr bil Couscous*)

Couscous has been popular in the Arabian Peninsula since Moroccan pilgrims began traveling to Mecca. Nowadays during the *hajj* season, hotels make a special effort to produce buffets for the pilgrims with foods from their homelands. Groups of American pilgrims enjoy a typical American meal, while groups from other countries enjoy foods from their native lands.

When I visited the city of Medina, I stayed at the Hilton next door to the Prophet Muhammad's mosque. A Turkish group and a Moroccan group were staying at the hotel along with our American group. For each meal, three different buffets were set up, each with foods from the three different countries. When guests entered the restaurant, the waiters asked to see their IDs and then led them, based on their nationalities, to the appropriate buffet. I love Moroccan food and was hoping I would be able to try it, instead of the typical American fare. Luckily, the waiter who was supposed to check my ID saw that I was wearing a Moroccan outfit and escorted me to the Moroccan buffet, which boasted many types of tajine and couscous. This is one of my favorite recipes.

Ingredients:
2 tablespoons olive oil
3 tablespoons butter, divided
2 pounds boneless and skinless chicken breast, sliced in half widthwise
1 medium onion, diced
1 teaspoon ground cinnamon
1 teaspoon green cardamom pods

1/2 teaspoon black pepper
1 teaspoon cumin
1 1/2 teaspoons saffron, divided
1/2 teaspoon chili powder
2 teaspoons cornstarch, dissolved in 2 cups chicken stock
1/2 pound dried dates, pitted
Juice of 1 lemon
2 cups couscous
Salt, to taste
1/2 cup roasted almonds, slivered

Preparation:

Heat oil and 2 tablespoons butter in a large skillet over medium-high heat. Sauté chicken pieces on each side until golden brown in color. Remove from pan and set aside.

Add onions, cinnamon, cardamom, black pepper, cumin, 1/2 teaspoon saffron, and chili pepper to skillet. Stir and sauté until onions are tender.

Return chicken to the skillet and add cornstarch and stock mix and dates. Stir and lower heat to medium low. Cover and simmer for 45 minutes, or until chicken is cooked through and dates are tender.

While chicken is simmering, prepare couscous: Bring 2 cups water and 1 teaspoon saffron to a boil, uncovered, in a medium saucepan with a lid. When water is boiling, remove pan from heat and add couscous. Mix well, cover pan with lid, and let stand for 5 to 10 minutes. Remove lid and add remaining 1 tablespoon butter. Stir, add salt, and fluff with a fork. Spoon couscous onto a large serving platter.

Remove cardamom pods from chicken tajine and arrange chicken on top of couscous. Sprinkle roasted almonds over the top. Serve immediately.

Serves 4 to 6.

Tip: If you would like to make this dish ahead of time, prepare the chicken tajine, allow it to cool completely, and store it in the refrigerator overnight. The next day it can be reheated while the couscous is being prepared.

Red Rice and Shrimp Skillet
(*Roz Ahmar bil Jamberi*)

Cooking the rice in beet juice gives it a ruby red color. The beets' flavor and color enhance this dish a great deal. When beets are not available, the rice can be prepared in water or broth.

Ingredients:
1/2 cup unbleached, all-purpose flour
1 1/2 teaspoons salt, divided
2 pounds shrimp, peeled and deveined*
4 cups basmati rice, rinsed and drained well
2 tablespoons butter
3 1/2 cups beet juice (reserved from making Beet Salad with
     Tahini Dressing, see page 12)
1 tablespoon Saudi Spice Mix (see page 3)
1/4 cup extra-virgin olive oil
1 onion, finely chopped
2 tablespoons fresh parsley, finely chopped

Preparation:
Spread flour and 1/2 teaspoon salt on a large platter. Coat
    shrimp with flour and set aside.

Place the rice in a large saucepan with butter, remaining 1
    teaspoon salt, beet juice, 2 cups water, and Saudi Spice
    Mix. Bring to a boil over high heat. Stir, reduce heat to
    low, and cover. Cook rice for 20 to 30 minutes, until
    water is absorbed, and rice is fluffy. Keep rice covered
    until ready to serve.

While rice is cooking, heat olive oil in a large skillet over
    medium-high heat. Add onions and fry until golden. Add
    the shrimp, taste, season with salt if needed, and sauté
    3 to 5 minutes per side until cooked through.

Spoon the cooked rice onto a serving platter. Top with

---

* To devein a shrimp, hold it with its back facing upward. Make a split down the length of the spine with a paring knife and remove the black thread.

shrimp and onions. Sprinkle parsley over the top. Serve immediately.

Serves 4 to 6.

Beef Makhtoum (Makhtoum)

This is another recipe in which the meat is marinated in yogurt for textural variance. *Makhtoum* was originally served throughout the Arabian Peninsula with mutton meat, but now beef *makhtoum* is also popular. Try serving it with plain rice and sautéed spinach to make a complete meal.

Ingredients:

1 tablespoon clarified butter (ghee)
1 large onion, diced
3/4 cup plain yogurt, drained well
1/2 cup crushed tomatoes or tomato puree
2 teaspoons Saudi Spice Mix (see page 3)
3 pounds boneless beef shoulder meat, cubed
Salt, to taste

Preparation:

Heat the clarified butter in a small saucepan over medium heat. Add the onion and sauté until lightly golden. Drain the onion and discard liquid.

Combine onion, yogurt, tomatoes or tomato puree, and Saudi Spice Mix in a large bowl and mix well. Add meat and turn well to coat. Cover and refrigerate 1 to 2 hours or overnight.

Heat a large saucepan over low heat and add marinated meat. Season with salt.

Cook, uncovered, for 1 1/2 to 2 hours, or until meat is very tender and sauce is thick. Serve warm.

Serves 6 to 8.

Tip: Marinate the meat the night before for extra flavor and to cut down on cooking time the next day. Make pita sandwiches out of leftovers by stuffing pitas with meat, shredded lettuce, and pickles.

Rose Cooler
(Assír Ward)

This is a delicious and refreshing rose-infused drink. Its color, taste, and floral content make it perfect for a romantic occasion. Be sure to use organic, untreated rose petals to garnish the drink. They can be purchased at most organic supermarkets and florists. The color can be best appreciated if this drink is served in small, clear punch or cocktail glasses.

Ingredients:
2 cups water, chilled
1 cup sugar
4 tablespoons lemon juice
10 drops red food coloring
1/2 cup rose water*
Organic rose petals, to garnish

Preparation:
Combine water, sugar, lemon juice, food coloring, and rose water in a pitcher. Stir well to incorporate all ingredients. Taste and adjust sugar, if necessary. Pour into a pitcher or glasses, and garnish with organic rose petals. Serve chilled.
Serves 4.

Golden Dream Cocktail
(Cocktail Helm mín Dahab)

Because the *Qur'an* prohibits the consumption of alcohol, the countries of the Arabian Peninsula have invented hundreds of fantastic fresh fruit cocktails to serve at celebrations. Throughout the Middle East, the quality and flavor of fresh fruit is superb, and juice bars and restaurants receive daily shipments of just-picked fruit. Usually the fruits are flavorful enough that they do not need to be sweetened. The taste of this cocktail is as special as its name.

---

* See "Where to Buy Guide" for purchasing information.

Ingredients:

Juice of 2 mandarin oranges*
1 teaspoon saffron, plus extra for garnish
2 cups whole milk
1 tablespoon honey
4 cups peach nectar

Preparation:

Place ingredients in a blender. Whip for 1 minute, or until
  ingredients are combined and top of cocktail is frothy.
  Taste and adjust honey if necessary. Pour cocktail into
  crystal glasses. Top each with a pinch of saffron. If not
  serving immediately, store juice in a pitcher in the refrigerator and shake well before serving.
Serves 4 to 6.

Sesame Ring Cookies
(Biskoweet bil Simsim)

These cookies are simple to make. Their crunchy exterior
and buttery filling are what make them popular. They're always
one of the first kinds of cookie to disappear from my cookie trays.
You can top them with poppy, rather than sesame, seeds, if you
prefer. If you do not like anise, you can substitute vanilla or almond extract.

Ingredients:

1/2 cup unsalted butter, at room temperature, plus extra for
  greasing
1/2 cup canola oil
1 cup confectioners' sugar
3 1/2 cups unbleached, all-purpose flour
1 tablespoon anise extract
1/2 cup whole milk
1 egg, slightly beaten
1/2 cup sesame seeds

---

* If mandarin oranges are not in season, substitute mandarin
   syrup from 1 (11-ounce) can of mandarin oranges.

Preparation:

Preheat oven to 350°F. Grease 2 baking sheets with butter.

Cream butter, canola oil, and confectioners' sugar in a large bowl. Stir in the flour, anise extract, and milk. Mix well to combine and form a dough ball.

Shape spoonfuls of dough into 1-inch balls. Roll the balls into ropes 3- to 4-inches long. Form a ring with the rope and press the ends to seal. Place rings 1 inch apart on cookie sheets. Brush tops of rings lightly with beaten egg and sprinkle with sesame seeds.

Bake on center rack for 15 to 20 minutes, or until cookies are golden. Cool on racks and serve.

Makes about 2 1/2 dozen.

**Tip: You can make Sesame Ring Cookies up to
a month in advance, freeze them,
and defrost them a few hours before serving.**

Mahlab Ring Cookies (Mahlabayat)

The windows of Arabian bakeries often showcase these cookies stacked high on enormous trays. *Mahlab*, a widely used ingredient in Middle Eastern cooking that is made from crushed cherry pits, is the star of these ring-shaped cookies. They can be stored in the freezer for up to one month and are wonderful additions to celebratory cookie trays.

Ingredients:

1/3 cup unsalted butter, melted
1/3 cup corn oil
1/2 cup sugar
4 cups unbleached, all-purpose flour
1 1/2 teaspoons baking powder
3 teaspoons *mahlab**

---

*   See "Where to Buy Guide" for purchasing information.

1/2 teaspoon salt
1 teaspoon anise extract

Preparation:
Preheat oven to 350°F.

Place the butter, corn oil, 1/2 cup water, and sugar in a large mixing bowl. Cream until everything is evenly incorporated. Add the flour, baking powder, mahlab, salt, and anise. Stir well to form a dough.

Shape spoonfuls of dough into balls. Place the balls 2 inches apart on ungreased cookie sheets. Press the balls flat and make a hole in the center with the base of a wooden spoon.

Bake 15 to 20 minutes until lightly golden. Remove from oven and cool on cookie sheets.

Makes about 4 dozen.

Tip: These cookies taste great with coffee at breakfast.

Almond-Stuffed Chocolate-Covered Dates (Tamr bil Lowz wa Chocolata)

Candy shops all over Saudi Arabia sell boxes of individually wrapped Almond-Stuffed Chocolate-Covered Dates. I was first introduced to them in Jeddah, where they were given to me as a gift. They make perfect party favors.

When choosing dates for this recipe, look for those that are slightly firm to the touch but not too hard. Most Medjool dates sold in major supermarkets work fine. Keep in mind that the amount this recipe yields will vary depending on the size and weight of the dates. Using a candy thermometer will ensure that the chocolate hardens properly.

Ingredients:
1 pound dried dates
3/4 cup blanched (skinless) almonds*

---

* If you cannot find blanched almonds, substitute roasted almonds instead.

10 ounces semi-sweet chocolate, broken into small pieces
3/4 cup heavy cream

Preparation:

Split each date lengthwise, being careful not to cut the dates
in half, and remove the pit. Stuff each date with an
almond. Press the seams of the split together to close
the date.

Melt chocolate in a double boiler over low heat. Be careful
not to let the water in the bottom of the boiler touch
the bottom of the top pan. Let the chocolate melt and
keep it over low heat until it reaches 113°F; check the
temperature with a candy thermometer. Remove the
pan of melted chocolate from heat. Set the warm pan
over a bowl of cool water to bring its temperature down
to 88°F.

Line the counter with wax paper, and place a cooling rack
on top of the paper.

Using tongs to handle the dates, dip each date into chocolate. Place chocolate covered dates on the cooling rack.
Cool dates 1 to 2 hours, or until chocolate is set. Transfer dates to a serving platter and store in the refrigerator until ready to use.

Makes about 2 dozen.

To make favors you will need:
Clear cellophane (3x4-inch) treat bags (1 for each date)
1 spool of craft ribbon, in the color of your choice, cut into 4-
inch strips (1 strip for each bag)
Small tags with strings to tie around the ribbon (1 for each
bag)

Directions:

Open each bag and carefully place a date inside. Twist the
bag and tie a ribbon around the bag, just above the
date, to seal. Write or type a message on each tag; this
could include the name of the bride and groom and the
date of the wedding. Tie the tag to the center of the
ribbons. Place favors on a serving platter.

Entertaining Timeline

Three months before the event:
Make guest list.
Send invitations.
Order a cake.
Order or purchase decorations for the event. White or red table linens will go nicely with the meal.

Two months before the event:
Order flowers, white for red table linens or red for white table linens.
Order an ice sculpture, if desired.
Buy, order, or borrow serving platters, a cake stand, and chaffing trays.
Choose Arabian music to play at the reception.

One month before the event:
Confirm the number of guests and adjust recipe quantities to match number of guests.
Make and freeze Sesame Ring Cookies and *Mahlab* Ring Cookies.
Buy specialty ingredients.
Make Sesame Chapati Bread and freeze.

One week before the event:
Order assorted pastries for guest tables.
Buy candies for guest tables.
Make and freeze Mini Swiss Chard Omelets and Cheese and Blessed Seed Turnovers.
Make Almond-Stuffed Chocolate-Covered Dates and store in refrigerator.
Buy all groceries except for meat, shrimp, and chicken.

Three days before the event:
Buy meat, shrimp, and chicken.
Double-check to make sure you don't have to double or increase recipe quantities.

Two days before the event:
Decorate reception area.
Re-read through recipes.
Make and refrigerate drinks.

One day before the event:
Remove appetizers and cookies from the freezer; move appetizers to the refrigerator.
Arrange cookies in mounds on platters and cover.
Make and refrigerate meat dumplings for soup.
Marinate leg of lamb.
Make Saudi Chicken and Date *Tajine* (couscous will be made the day of the event).
Make Beet Salad with Tahini Dressing (be sure to reserve cooking water to prepare red rice tomorrow)
Make Beef *Makhtoum* (beef portion only)

Day of the event:
Roast leg of lamb.
Garnish Mini Swiss Chard Omelets with *Labna*.
Make soup for Meat Dumplings in Consommé.
Set up dessert portion of buffet.
Set guest tables with flowers, chocolates, and assorted pastries.
Make Red Rice and Shrimp Skillet.
Make Eggplant, Tomato, and Chili Pepper Salad.
Make saffron couscous for Saudi Chicken and Date *Tajine*.

One hour before the event:
Set up appetizer and salad portion of buffet.
Place all hot items in chaffing dishes on buffet.
Begin playing music.

CHAPTER 2
Eid Feast

Holiday celebrations in the Arabian Peninsula are well-orchestrated events in which the whole community takes part. *Eid* is the Arabic world for holiday. The two important *Eids* of the Muslim calendar are the *Eid al Fitr*, which is a three-day holiday that comes at the end of Ramadan, and the *Eid al Adha*, or the Feast of the Sacrifice, a four-day holiday that comes at the end of the annual pilgrimage to Mecca. I had the pleasure of spending the *Eid al Adha* in the guest palace in Mina, Saudi Arabia.

Mina is an ancient city where the Prophet Abraham once lived. According to Islamic history, one night Abraham dreamed that God ordered him to sacrifice his son Ishmael. Although the thought of sacrificing his own son caused Abraham great stress, he knew he had to obey God's wishes. Ishmael understood his father's sorrow and gave Abraham permission to sacrifice him. When Ishmael was about to be killed, the archangel Gabriel appeared to Abraham and told him that his dream was only a test of his faith and that God did not want him to kill his son. Gabriel ordered Abraham to sacrifice a sheep instead.

Every year Muslims celebrate the *Eid al Adha* by sacrificing sheep. When a sheep is sacrificed, the name of God is pronounced upon it. After it is butchered, its meat is divided into thirds. One third of the meat is given to the poor, another third is given to the extended family of the person who purchased it, and the last third is kept for the immediate family of the person who purchased it. Needless to say, lamb recipes abound at *Eid al Adha* tables. In Saudi Arabia, neighbors congregate to prepare whole lambs, which are stuffed with chickens that have, in turn, been stuffed with savory rice pilaf.

When I spent the holiday at the guest palace in Mina, a sumptuous buffet including hundreds of dishes was prepared for King Abdullah's guests. Tables full of appetizers, soups and breads, main courses, salads, special desserts, and fresh fruits were offered. The menu that follows includes some of my favorites from this feast. Keep in mind that the buffet can be altered to fit many different seasons and occasions.

The theme color for this event is the Prophet Muhammad's favorite color, green, which Muslims call "the color of heaven." For religious regions mentioned earlier, lamb is prominent in the menu items. When greeting guests, it is polite to wish them a happy holiday by saying "*Eid Mubarak*" or by writing the same phrase on place cards and invitations.

Inside the Great Mosque in Medina, Saudi Arabia.

Menu
Appetizers:
Classic Arabian Hummus (Hommus bil Tahina)
Spinach Triangles (Fatayer bil Sabanikh)
Assorted Pickles (purchased)
Assorted Olives (purchased)
Pita Bread (purchased)
Soup:
Fragrant Vermicelli Soup (Hasaa bil Shareya)

Spice-Infused Stock (Hasaa)
Salads:
Mixed Salad (Salata Khadra)
Cucumber and Yogurt Salad (Salata Khoyar bil Laban)
Main Courses:
Rice with Lamb Filet, Peas, and Nuts (Ouzi)
Fish with Saffron Béchamel (Samak bil Saffran wa
Béchamel)
Chicken Kabobs (Shish Tawook)
Lamb Stew with Peas and Cauliflower (Tajin Lahma
Dani bil Bisella wa Arnabit)
Drink:
Pomegranate and Berry Cooler (Cocktail bi Ruman wa
Frawila)
Desserts:
Mango Milk Pudding (Mahallibeya bil Manga)
Baklava Parcels (Sannadiq Ba'lawa)

Classic Arabian Hummus (*Hommus bil Tahina*)

This creamy chickpea puree was featured at every meal I ate in Saudi Arabia. Whether I was in Mecca, Medina, or Jeddah, at someone's home, in a restaurant, or at the king's guest palace, hummus was always present. Despite its constant availability, I never tired of eating it.

Interestingly, the word *hommus* means "chickpeas" in Arabic. The real name for this dish is *Hommus bil Tahina*, or "chickpeas with sesame paste" in English.

Ingredients:
1 cup cooked or canned chickpeas, peeled*
1 garlic clove, minced

---

* To peel chickpeas, hold them in between your thumb and index finger over a bowl and squeeze. The chickpea will come through so that you will be left with only the skin in your hand. I like to peel chickpeas while I'm watching television or talking on the phone, and leave them ready in the refrigerator, so that I can make this dish in minutes whenever I want it.

1/3 cup tahini (sesame paste)
1/8 cup extra-virgin olive oil, plus 2 teaspoons for garnish
Salt, to taste
Dash of cayenne pepper, to taste
Dash of paprika, for garnish

Preparation:

Place chickpeas in a food processor, reserving a few for gar-
    nish. Add the remaining ingredients, except for paprika
    and 2 teaspoons olive oil, to the food processor. Puree
    until smooth. Add water, a tablespoon at a time, to get
    an extra creamy consistency (you should need less than
    1/4 cup in total). Scrape down the sides of the food pro-
    cessor, and puree for 1 to 2 additional minutes. Taste
    and adjust seasonings as necessary.
If not serving immediately, store in a container with a lid in
    the refrigerator. Otherwise, spoon into a small round
    dish. Using the back of a spoon, make 4 to 6 dents in
    the top of the hummus and fill the dents with the re-
    maining olive oil. Sprinkle with paprika and arrange
    remaining chickpeas on the top. Serve with warm pita.
Serves 4.

Spinach Triangles (*Fatayer bil Sabanikh*)

Fatayer are tender bread triangles that can be stuffed with
a variety of ingredients. They can be found in bakeries, street-
side stalls, and home kitchens. They are a delightful snack to
enjoy anytime but are served as special appetizers for holiday
occasions as well.

Ingredients:

For the bread:
1 tablespoon active dry yeast
2 cups unbleached, all-purpose flour
2 teaspoons extra-virgin olive oil, divided
1/2 teaspoon salt
For the filling:
1 cup frozen chopped spinach, thawed and drained well
1 grated onion, drained well

Juice of 1 lemon
2 tablespoons fresh mint, chopped
2 tablespoons extra-virgin olive oil
Salt, to taste

Preparation:

To make dough, combine yeast with 1/4 cup tepid water in a large mixing bowl. Add flour, 1 teaspoon olive oil, and salt. Mix until blended. Add 1/3 cup water, a little at a time, until dough is smooth.

Spinach Triangles

Turn dough out onto a lightly floured work surface. Knead dough until it is smooth and elastic (5 to 10 minutes).

Oil another large bowl with remaining teaspoon of olive oil. Place dough in bowl and turn to coat with olive oil. Cover with a kitchen cloth and let rise in a warm place for 1 hour, or until doubled.

Preheat the oven to 350°F. Line 2 cookie sheets with parchment paper or grease with butter or oil.

Take dough out of the bowl and place on a lightly floured work surface. Lightly dust the top of the dough and a rolling pin with flour. Roll out the dough to approximately 1/8-inch thickness. Cut out 24 (3-inch) circles from the dough (the floured rim of a glass can be used for this).

To make filling, combine all of the stuffing ingredients in a medium bowl. Stir to incorporate all ingredients well.

Fill each dough circle with 1 scant teaspoon of filling. Fill a small bowl with water and keep it next to the dough. Dip your fingers in the water and wet the outer edges of the dough circle. Fold the bottom half of the circle up to the middle. Pinch in the top two sides of the circle to form a triangle. If the dough does not seal easily, use more water to coat the edges.

Place 12 triangles on each cookie sheet, leaving space between each one. Bake for 20 to 30 minutes, until golden brown, making sure not to open the oven during the first 10 minutes of baking. Serve warm.

Makes about 2 dozen.

Tip: *If you are making the* fatayer *in advance, allow them to cool before storing them in an airtight container. They can be frozen for up to one month.*

Fragrant Vermicelli Soup (*Hasaa bil Shareya*)

This quick soup is a common first course for both everyday and holiday occasions in the Middle East. Most people make this soup from the stock of whatever meat they are cooking for dinner that day. If you do not have time to make homemade stock, substitute your favorite boxed or canned variety. For a less spicy soup, omit the hot peppers. You can also use orzo instead of the vermicelli.

Ingredients:
8 cups Spice-Infused Stock (see page 31)
1 tablespoon tomato paste
2 hot green peppers, diced
Salt, to taste
1 cup vermicelli
1 lime, cut into 6 slices
Fresh cilantro or parsley to garnish

Preparation:
Bring broth to a boil in a large stockpot. Add tomato paste and peppers, and stir well. Add salt, to taste. Add vermicelli and stir well. Turn heat down to low and simmer until vermicelli is done, about 7 to 10 minutes.

Garnish with fresh cilantro or parsley. Serve hot with lime slices.

Serves 6.

Tip: Add leftover chicken or turkey meat and frozen peas and carrots to this soup to make a quick dinner.

Spice-Infused Stock (Hasaa)

Making your own stock at home allows you to control the amount of sodium you consume. Using a unique blend of spices when making broth can both personalize and enhance the taste of a soup. I like to use fennel stalks and dried rosebuds to give my stock a unique flavor. They can be omitted, if preferred.

Ingredients:
5 green cardamom pods
2 peppercorns
1 cinnamon stick
1 teaspoon dried organic rosebuds* (if desired)
1 dried lemon
1 dried lime
2 pieces meat with bone attached (beef, lamb, chicken, or veal)
1 onion, roughly chopped
1 carrot, roughly chopped
1 celery stick, roughly chopped
stalks of 1 fennel bulb (reserve bulb for another use)
2 tablespoons salt, or to taste

Preparation:
Fill an 8-quart stockpot 3/4 of the way full with water.
Combine cardamom pods, peppercorns, cinnamon stick, and rosebuds in a piece of cheesecloth and tie with butcher's twine to seal. (These ingredients may also be added to the pot loose; the stock will be strained later.) Add spice bag to the pot with dried lemon, dried lime, meat, onion, carrot, celery, and fennel. Add salt, stir, and bring to a boil over high heat. Skim scum off the top with a

*   See "Where to Buy Guide" for purchasing information
    for rosebuds, dried lemon, and dried lime.

slotted spoon as it forms. Reduce heat to low and simmer for 2 to 3 hours.

Strain stock into another container and discard spices and
vegetables. The meat may be reserved for another use.

Unused stock may be refrigerated for up to a week or frozen
for up to a month.

Makes about 6 quarts.

**Tip: Because this recipe makes several quarts of stock, you
will likely want to freeze the leftovers in a combination of
single- and family-serving-size freezer containers to use at
another time.**

Mixed Salad
(Salata Khadra)

This simple salad is the perfect addition to most Arabian
meals.

Ingredients:

6 small (3- to 4-inch) cucumbers, diced
4 tomatoes, diced
1 bunch fresh parsley, stems removed and chopped
1 small onion, grated and drained
Juice of 1 lemon
1/4 cup extra-virgin olive oil
Salt, to taste
Freshly ground pepper, to taste

Preparation:

Place first 4 ingredients in a large salad bowl.

Whisk lemon juice and olive oil together in a small bowl.
Season with salt and pepper to taste.

Combine dressing with salad and toss to combine.

Serves 4 to 6.

**Tip: You can prepare this salad a day ahead of time. Keep it
in the refrigerator overnight, and toss with dressing before
serving.**

Cucumber and Yogurt Salad
(Salata Khoyar bil Laban)

I love Cucumber and Yogurt Salad so much that I often eat it for breakfast.

Ingredients:

3 cups plain whole yogurt, drained well
6 small cucumbers, diced and drained, or 1 regular cucumber
1 tablespoon dried mint, if desired
Salt, to taste

Preparation:

Place yogurt in a medium-size bowl. Add cucumbers, and
  stir. Add dried mint, and season with salt to taste. Serve
  immediately to prevent salad from becoming runny.
Serves 4 to 6.

Tip: You can use this salad as a dip for fresh vegetables.

Rice with Lamb Filet, Peas, and Nuts
(Ouzi)

Ouzi is prepared in hundreds of different ways across the Arabian Peninsula. Lamb, rice, and various spices are the common denominators in all of the recipes. This version is easy to make and can be eaten alone or with a salad on any occasion.

Ingredients:

3 tablespoons olive oil, divided
1/4 cup pine nuts
1/2 cup pistachios, skinned and chopped
1 small onion, diced
1 pound lamb filet, cut into 1/2-inch cubes
1 1/2 cups basmati rice, rinsed, soaked in water for 20 minutes, and drained
2 1/2 cups vegetable or chicken stock
1 teaspoon ground cinnamon
Salt, to taste
Freshly ground pepper, to taste

1/2 cup frozen peas, thawed
1/4 cup raisins

Preparation:
Heat 2 tablespoons oil in a large saucepan over medium heat. Add nuts, stir, and fry until they begin to color and release their aroma. Using a slotted spoon, remove nuts from the oil.

Add the remaining tablespoon of oil. Add onion to the pan and sauté until it is translucent, 3 to 5 minutes. Add lamb meat and brown on all sides. Add rice, stock, cinnamon, salt, and pepper, and stir to incorporate well. Increase heat to high and bring to a boil. Stir and reduce heat to the lowest setting possible. Allow to cook for 20 to 30 minutes, or until all liquid is absorbed.

Remove lid, take off flame, and carefully stir in nuts, peas, and raisins. Place lid back on the pan to keep *ouzi* warm until serving. If not serving immediately, wrap towels around the saucepan to prevent heat from escaping.

If rice cools before it is time to serve, heat saucepan over a larger pan filled with hot water to touch the bottom of the rice pan until rice becomes warm again, or place the rice pan directly over a low flame to reheat.

Serves 4 to 6.

Tip: When frying the nuts, be careful to cook them only until they exude their aroma because if they are cooked too long they will burn once they are taken off the heat. There is a proverb in the Arab world that cooking nuts is like rearing children: "you can never turn your backs on them."

Fish with Saffron Béchamel
(Samak bil Saffran wa Béchamel)
Béchamel sauce is a popular indulgence in the Arabian Peninsula. In this version saffron, a spice the Arabians originally imported from India, is added to the traditional French sauce, which is served over fresh fish from the Red Sea. Any fresh, firm-fleshed white fish works well for this dish. Cod, orange roughy,

bass, and rockfish work very well. The béchamel sauce can be made in advance, kept in the refrigerator, and poured over the fish just before baking.

Ingredients:
For the sauce:
3 tablespoons unsalted butter
3 tablespoons flour
2 cups whole milk, heated
Salt, to taste
Freshly ground pepper, to taste
1 teaspoon good quality saffron
For the fish:
5 tablespoons olive oil, divided
Zest and juice of 1 lemon
1 teaspoon ground cinnamon
1/2 teaspoon freshly ground black pepper
1/2 teaspoon ground coriander
2 pounds fresh white fish fillets
1 onion, sliced
1 cup grated Romano cheese

Preparation:
To make sauce, melt the butter in a saucepan over medium heat. Whisk in the flour and cook, stirring until blended, for 1 minute, or until mixture is light golden. Gradually add the milk, whisking constantly. Continue to whisk until the sauce is smooth and slightly thickened, about 5 to 7 minutes. Add the salt, pepper, and saffron and stir. Raise the heat and simmer for a few minutes. Taste and adjust salt and pepper if needed. Set aside until ready to use. If making the sauce in advance, allow it to cool and store it overnight in an airtight container in the refrigerator.

Combine 3 tablespoons of olive oil with lemon zest and juice, cinnamon, black pepper, and coriander in a large shallow baking dish. Place fish fillets in dish and turn to coat. Scatter onions on top and cover with plastic wrap and place in the refrigerator to marinate for 1 hour.

In the meantime, preheat the oven to 400°F.

After fish has marinated for 1 hour, remove it from the refrigerator and top with saffron béchamel. Top with Romano cheese and bake, uncovered, for 15 to 20 minutes until bubbly and fish is cooked through.

Serves 4 to 6.

Tip: *Bake thinly sliced potatoes and small broccoli florets alongside the fish for a quick meal in a pan.*

Kabobs

Chicken Kabobs (*Shish Tawook*)

Kabobs are popular street fare throughout the Middle East. They can be bought virtually anywhere and are made from chicken, beef, veal, and lamb. They are also served in restaurants with rice and salad. For formal buffets, kabob skewers are pushed into carved melons or arranged in glass containers with the pointed end sticking up to form meat "bouquets."

Ingredients:
1/4 cup olive oil
2 garlic cloves, minced

Juice and zest of 2 lemons
Pinch of saffron
Salt, to taste
Freshly ground pepper, to taste
2 pounds chicken breast meat, skinned and cubed
1 teaspoon ground cumin

Preparation:

Combine olive oil, garlic, lemon juice and zest, saffron, salt, and pepper in a large bowl. Stir the mixture and add the chicken cubes, mixing to coat all pieces of chicken well. Cover and marinate for 1 hour at room temperature or overnight in the refrigerator.

Prepare 4 long or 8 short skewers.*

Thread the chicken pieces onto a skewer by piercing each chicken piece through the bottom. Avoid pushing the meat too close together; cubes should be touching, but not crowded, to ensure even cooking. Sprinkle cumin on top of each skewer.

If using a grill, place skewers directly on a prepared grill for 7 to 10 minutes on each side until chicken is cooked through. If using a broiler, preheat broiler and place skewers onto a baking sheet. Broil for 7 to 10 minutes on each side, or until chicken is cooked through. Remove from broiler and wrap in layers of aluminum foil to keep kabobs warm.

Serves 4 to 6.

Tip: You can make double the quantity of Chicken Kabobs and use the extra chicken for making a salad the next day.

Lamb Stew with Peas and Cauliflower (Tajin Lahma Dani bil Bisella wa Arnabit)

This comforting stew was served to us at the palace in Mecca, Saudi Arabia. It tastes great with rice or couscous and can be made ahead of time. Frozen cauliflower may be substituted for

---

* If using wooden skewers, soak them in water for 30 minutes to prevent them from burning. Metal skewers need no preparation.

fresh, and beef can be used instead of lamb. This stew can be made in advance and frozen for up to a month.

Ingredients:
2 tablespoons olive oil
1 onion, roughly chopped
2 pounds boneless lamb shoulder, cubed
1 tablespoon Saudi Spice Mix (see page 3)
1 cup chicken stock
1 cup chopped tomatoes
1 cup cauliflower flowerets
1 cup green peas
Salt, to taste

Preparation:
Heat oil in a medium saucepan over medium heat. Add onion and sauté until translucent. Add meat and brown on all sides. Season with Saudi Spice Mix and stir. Add chicken stock, increase heat to high, and bring to a boil. Reduce heat to medium low, stir, cover, and simmer for 1 1/2 hours, until meat is tender.

Add tomatoes, vegetables, and salt, stir, cover, and let simmer for 30 minutes until tender. Taste and adjust seasonings if necessary.

Serves 4 to 6.

Pomegranate and Berry Cooler (Cocktail bi Ruman wa Frawila)

This is a light, refreshing cooler that can be served on any occasion. Pomegranates are coveted in the Middle East for their taste, beauty, and nutritional properties. Traditional Arabian poetry often described the cheeks or lips of a loved one as being pomegranate colored.

Pomegranate juice has been proved to help prevent cardiovascular disease. Claudio Napoli, medical professor at the University of Naples, Italy, states, "We have established the polyphenols (antioxidant chemicals) and other natural compounds contained in pomegranate juice may retard artherogenesis (the hardening of the arteries)."

Ingredients:
1 bottle sparkling water, chilled
1/2 cup sugar-free pomegranate juice
3/4 cup strawberry syrup
4 to 6 teaspoons sugar
1/2 cup fresh strawberries

Preparation:
Mix sparkling water, pomegranate juice, strawberry syrup, and sugar together in a pitcher with a wooden spoon. Taste and adjust sugar, if necessary.

Divide strawberries and place inside champagne flutes. Pour juice over the strawberries in each flute. Serve immediately.

Serves 4 to 6.

Mango Milk Pudding (*Mahallibeya bil Manga*)

Mahallibeya is the smooth and creamy pudding tradition-ally made with rice flour. It is usually served alone and is a Middle Eastern classic. This recipe adds delicious mango pieces to the pudding for a sweet, unexpected, twist. Do not use a metal whisk to prepare this recipe, as the metal will cause the pudding to separate.

Ingredients:
3 cups milk
1/2 cup sugar
1 teaspoon rose water
3 1/2 tablespoons cornstarch
1 cup fresh mango, cut into 1-inch pieces
1/2 cup whipped cream, for garnish
1/4 cup ground almonds, blanched

Preparation:
Pour milk into a medium saucepan and add sugar and rose water. Heat, uncovered, over medium heat until boil-ing, stirring constantly.

Mix cornstarch with 1/4 cup water. Slowly add cornstarch mixture to the saucepan and whisk vigorously. Boil pudding for 2 minutes, stirring, and reduce heat to low. Continue stirring and cook until thick, 15 to 20 minutes. When the pudding has reduced to at least 1/2 of its original volume, set it aside to cool.

Pour the pudding into individual custard bowls. Cover the tops with mango pieces. Refrigerate until pudding sets. To serve, garnish with dollops of whipped cream and ground almonds.

Serves 6 to 8.

Tip: You can use this smooth pudding as a topping for sponge or pound cake.

Baklava Parcels (*Sannadiq Ba'lawa*)

This is a simple and authentic way to prepare classic baklava. Keep in mind that when you go to a Middle Eastern or Greek grocer to buy phyllo dough, the dough will be available in different thicknesses. I like to use #7, which is slightly thicker than #4. You may use whichever you prefer for this recipe. Also, phyllo dough needs to be thawed according to package instructions before it can be used.

Ingredients:
For the syrup:
2 cups sugar
1 cup water
1 teaspoon lemon juice
1 teaspoon orange blossom water
1 teaspoon rose water
For the filling:
2 cups ground walnuts
4 tablespoons sugar
For the baklava:
1 box phyllo dough, thawed
1 cup clarified butter (ghee)

Preparation:
To make syrup, combine sugar, water, and lemon juice in a medium saucepan. Bring mixture to a boil over medium

heat, stirring until sugar dissolves. Once sugar is dissolved, stop stirring and reduce heat to low. Simmer 10 to 15 minutes, until syrup is thick. Remove from heat, stir in orange blossom and rose water, and cool.

To make filling, stir nuts and sugar together in a medium-size bowl.

Position oven rack in the center of oven. Preheat oven to 350°F.

To make baklava, remove phyllo from package and place on a work surface. Separate one piece at a time, place on a work surface, and brush the top of each piece with clarified butter to cover. Continue buttering and stacking until you have 10 sheets on top of each other.

Cut the dough into 4x4-inch squares. Place a tablespoon of ground nuts in the center of each square. Gather the 4 sides of the square in toward the middle without closing the square, pinching the corners together. If corners do not stay sealed, brush with more clarified butter. Push the sides in to create a wider opening at the top.

Place parcels on ungreased baking sheets. Repeat the stacking, cutting, and filling until all phyllo is used.

Bake the parcels until golden, about 40 to 50 minutes. Rotate the baking sheets every 15 minutes to ensure even browning.

When finished baking, remove from oven, and pour the syrup over the baklava. Serve at room temperature and store leftovers in the refrigerator for up to 3 days.

Serves 8 to 10.

Tip: You can make the syrup in advance and store it in an airtight container in the refrigerator for up to 1 month.

Entertaining Timeline

One month before the event:
Invite friends and family to your feast.
Decide on the final menu.
Purchase green tablecloths and napkins.
Write a holiday greeting on place cards for each guest.

Two weeks before the event:
Confirm the number of guests, and adjust the recipe quantities appropriately.
Make grocery list.
Purchase groceries with a long shelf life (e.g., pickles, olives, canned chickpeas, vermicelli, rice, phyllo dough, mint extract, etc.).

One week before the event:
Finish grocery shopping.
Make Spinach Triangles and freeze.

Two days before the event:
Make Classic Arabian Hummus and store in the refrigerator.
Purchase fresh flowers for tables.

One day before the event:
Make saffron béchamel for Fish with Saffron Béchamel and store in refrigerator.
Marinate Chicken Kabobs.
Make Lamb Stew with Peas and Cauliflower and store in refrigerator.
Make Mango Milk Pudding and store in refrigerator.
Make Baklava Parcels.
Set tables with green linens, place cards, and fresh flowers.

Day of the event:
Remove Spinach Triangles from the freezer to thaw.
Remove Classic Arabian Hummus from the refrigerator and bring to room temperature.

Make Pomegranate and Berry Cooler and store in the refrigerator.

Make Cucumber and Yogurt Salad and store in the refrigerator.

Make Mixed Salad and store in the refrigerator.

Arrange Baklava Parcels on a dessert platter.

Arrange fresh strawberries on a serving platter with a bowl of whipped cream.

Three hours before the event:

Make Rice with Lamb Filet, Peas, and Nuts.

Make Fish with Saffron Béchamel.

Finish Chicken Kabobs.

Make Fragrant Vermicelli Soup.

One hour before the event:

Preheat oven to 350°F and heat Spinach Triangles, if desired.

Reheat Lamb Stew with Peas and Cauliflower and any other items that have gotten cold.

Serve Pomegranate and Berry Cooler and appetizers to guests when they arrive.

When everyone is seated, serve the soup, and begin placing main courses and salads on the tables.

CHAPTER 3
Arabian Tea Party

Arabian tea parties exude hospitality, elegance, and sweetness. The act of drinking tea is one of the most important social events of daily life in the Arabian Peninsula. In the palaces of Mecca and Jeddah, tea is available to guests throughout the day. It is served on sparkling silver trays and accompanied by small bowls of fresh mint leaves, sugar, and cream. In coffee shops, waiters will ask you how much sugar you would like when you order, and the tea will be served to you already sweetened.

Tea party hosts will go out of their way to make sure that your every need is attended to, without you having to ask for anything. Though Arabians traditionally drink loose-leaf black tea, hosts will offer you a variety of choices. Black, green, and imported brands like Lipton are typical offerings. While I was in Saudi Arabia, I was invited to a friend's home in Jeddah late one Friday evening. Our hostess knew that we had just attended a large buffet meal at the palace and were not hungry, and we reminded her when we arrived that we couldn't possibly eat anything else. "Why don't you prepare tea?" her husband asked. After we socialized for a few minutes we were offered trays of various types of tea, traditional Saudi *Mamoul* (date dome) cookies, fresh fruit and dates, pound cake, chocolate-covered dates and raisins, and assorted mixed nuts.

The tea party is the one of the easiest and least time-consuming entertaining ideas in the book. Although the game plan suggests that you start preparing a month in advance, the party could be pulled together in a few days, provided that you do not need to mail order any ingredients. If you think you will be holding an Arabian Tea Party in the future, it's a good idea to purchase the dried organic rosebuds, rose water, and orange blossom water now, so that you'll have them when you need them. All of the items for this party are made in advance, so you'll be able to enjoy your guests' company.

Use this menu to create a special occasion out of an ordinary day. Whether catching up with a friend or relative, entertaining out-of-town guests, or celebrating a shower, birthday, or anniversary, an Arabian Tea Party will make your guests feel special.

The theme for the Arabian Tea Party is the rose. Pink-colored table linens, teas made from dried rosebuds, desserts made with rose water, and serving trays decorated with fresh pink roses create a soft, romantic mood. Bottles of rose water are given to each guest as party favors. Place markers are single fresh pink roses that have guests' names tied to them. The music should be soft, instrumental, and romantic.

An Old Arabian Tea Story

At the market, every day many years ago, a young man passed an old man, and every time he passed the old man, the young man smiled, nodded his head, and greeted him. The old man never once replied. After a few months had gone by, the young man decided to approach the old man. He said, "Each day I pass you at the market, and each day I greet you. You've never greeted me once. Where are your manners? What do you have to lose by greeting me in return?"

"I have a lot to lose," said the old man. The young man insisted on a more specific explanation. "You see my son," said the old man, "if I say hello to you, you will continue to greet me each day. Eventually you will sit down and talk to me. After a pleasant chat, I will be obliged to offer you to visit me in my home. When you come to visit me at my home, I must offer you tea, as our custom dictates. Then, once you taste the delicious tea, you will inquire as to who made it. Then I will need to introduce you to my beautiful daughter. Once you see her, you will certainly ask me for her hand in marriage. So you see, my son, I do have a lot to lose by saying hello to you."

The old man never spoke to the young man again.

Menu
Drinks:
Black Tea (*Shai*)
Rosebud Tea (*Shai bil Ward*)

Chai with Cardamom, Cinnamon, and Ginger (*Shai bi Khail, Jinzabil, w'irfa*)

Desserts:
Semolina Squares with Yogurt (*Na'amoura*)
Cream-filled Phyllo Triangles (*Sha'bayat*)
Rose and Mint Infused Fruit Salad (*Salata bil Fakha, Ward, wa Na'na*)
Saudi Shortbread Cookies (*Ghorayeba*)
Assorted Dried Dates (purchased)
Mixed Nuts (purchased)

Black Tea (*Shai*)

Arabians prefer special blends of Ceylon teas, which are renown for their golden hue and strong flavor. The exact ingredients in each blend are kept a secret. They are known to be the highest quality and can be enjoyed anytime of day. For breakfast, Arabians serve glasses of half black tea and half warm milk. Remember to ask your guests weather they would like one, two, or three teaspoons of sugar, and to add the sweetener to the hot tea before you serve it. Black tea is usually served in short clear glasses in restaurants and coffee shops or in fine porcelain in homes.

Ingredients:
4 teaspoons high-quality loose-leaf black tea
4 cups boiling water
Sugar, if desired
Milk, if desired

Preparation:
Place tea in boiling water and add sugar. Cover, and allow to steep for 10 minutes for strong tea or 5 minutes for regular strength. Strain and serve warm.
Makes 4 cups.

Rosebud Tea (*Shai bil Ward*)

Rosebud Tea is a smooth, sophisticated drink made with dried organic rosebuds. Bags of dried rosebuds can be purchased from Middle Eastern markets (see the "Where to Buy Guide" for details). Some Bedouins add cinnamon sticks, saffron, and the leaves of dried dessert plants to their rose petals when making this drink. Sometimes, I enjoy the rose petals all by themselves. Use your finest china for this delicate beverage.

Ingredients:
4 teaspoons dried organic rosebuds
4 teaspoons rose water
4 cups boiling water
Sugar, if desired

Preparation:
Steep rosebuds and rose water, covered, in boiling water for
    five minutes. Strain, and serve hot with sugar, if desired.
Makes 4 cups.

Chai with Cardamom, Cinnamon, and Ginger (Shai bil Khail, Jinzabil, w'irfa)

Pakistani waiters in Jeddah, Saudi Arabia, prepared this delicious tea for us. They claimed its spices help to cure the common cold. For breakfast, it is served with warm milk.

Ingredients:
4 teaspoon high-quality loose-leaf Ceylon tea
4 green cardamom pods
4 teaspoons ground ginger
4 cinnamon sticks
4 cups boiling water
Honey, if desired
Milk, if desired

Preparation:
Combine tea and spices in boiling water. Cover and let steep
    for 10 minutes. Strain and add honey, if desired. Serve
    warm with milk, if desired.
Makes 4 cups.

Semolina Squares with Yogurt (Na'amoura)

Variations of this dessert can be found throughout the Middle East. This version is barely sweet enough to be considered a dessert. If you tend to like sugary desserts, increase the amount of sugar to 1 cup. Keep in mind that the semolina dough needs to be refrigerated for a minimum of 5 hours before baking. I like to make the dough the night before I'm serving the squares. Semolina squares will stay fresh for 2 to 3 days in the refrigerator.

Ingredients:
For the syrup:
2 cups sugar
1 cup water
Juice of 1 lemon
2 strips lemon peel
For the batter:
2 tablespoons tahini (sesame paste)
2 cups plain yogurt, drained well
2 cups semolina*
1/2 cup sugar
1 teaspoon orange blossom water
1 teaspoon rose water
2 teaspoons baking powder
1/4 cup blanched almonds, slivered

Preparation:
To make the syrup, combine all ingredients in a medium saucepan. Bring to a boil over medium heat, while stirring. Once sugar is dissolved, stop stirring and reduce heat to low. Allow syrup to simmer 10 to 15 minutes until thickened. Remove syrup from heat and cool. When syrup is cool, remove lemon peel.

Preheat oven to 375°F. Grease a medium (7x10-inch) baking dish with tahini.

To make batter, combine yogurt, semolina, sugar, orange blossom water, rose water, and baking powder in a large bowl. Mix to combine well and pour into prepared baking dish. Smooth out the top and cut into even-sized

---

*   See "Where to Buy Guide" for purchasing information.

squares. Press an almond sliver into the top of each square. Cover and refrigerate a minimum of 5 hours or a maximum of overnight.

Bake for 45 to 55 minutes, or until golden. The squares are done when they begin to pull away from the sides of the pan.

Top with half of the syrup. When the syrup is absorbed, pour on the remaining half of syrup.

Serve at room temperature. Store leftovers in refrigerator for up to 2 days.

Serves 10.

Tip: Make the syrup up to a month in advance and store it in an airtight container in the refrigerator.

Cream-filled Phyllo Triangles (Sha'bayat)

The word *sha'bayat* is a derivative of the plural form of the Arabic word for "popular." Once you make these delicious treats, you'll understand that they truly merit their name. I've yet to meet someone who doesn't love them. The tender, flaky phyllo triangles in this dessert are filled with a unique semolina cream that contains just the right amount of sweetness.

Burmese children in Mecca, Saudi Arabia

Ingredients:
For the filling:
2 cups whole milk
2 tablespoons sugar
5 tablespoons cornstarch, dissolved in 1/4 cup milk
1 cup heavy cream
1/4 cup semolina
1 tablespoon orange blossom water
1 tablespoon rose water

For the syrup:
2 cups sugar
1 cup water
1 teaspoon lemon juice
1 teaspoon orange blossom water
1 teaspoon rose water
For the phyllo triangles:
1 (16-ounce) package phyllo dough, thawed according to
 package directions
3/4 cup clarified butter (ghee), melted
1/4 cup ground pistachios, for garnish

Preparation:

To make the filling, combine milk and sugar in a medium
 saucepan over medium-high heat. Bring to a slow boil,
 stirring, and add the cornstarch-milk mixture. Whisk
 continuously until thickened. Reduce heat to low. Stir
 in cream, semolina, orange blossom water, and rose
 water. Continue to cook and stir for 2 more minutes.
 Set filling aside to cool.

Preheat oven to 400°F. Grease 2 baking sheets with clarified butter.

To make the syrup, combine the sugar, water, and lemon
 juice in a medium saucepan over medium heat. Bring
 to a boil and stir until sugar dissolves. Once sugar is
 dissolved, stop stirring and reduce heat to low. Simmer
 for 10 to 15 minutes until thickened. Remove from heat
 and set aside to cool.

To make the phyllo triangles remove the phyllo dough from
 the package. Set each piece on a work surface and
 brush it with clarified butter. Continue stacking and
 brushing each sheet with butter until you have 10 sheets
 stacked. Cut the stacked phyllo into 4-inch squares with
 a sharp knife or pizza cutter. Put the cream on one side
 of each square. Brush the borders of each square with
 additional clarified butter. Fold the empty half of the
 phyllo over on the diagonal to cover the cream and
 form a triangle. Press down on the edges to seal in
 the cream.

Place 6 triangles on each baking sheet. Bake for 10 minutes, rotate pans, brush with more clarified butter, and bake for 15 to 20 more minutes, or until golden. Remove from oven and pour syrup evenly over the tops of each triangle.

Allow phyllo triangles to cool, and garnish with pistachios. Serve warm or at room temperature.

The triangles may be stored in the refrigerator for 2 to 3 days. Reheat them for 10 to 20 seconds in the microwave before serving.

Makes approximately 12.

Tip: To save time, make the cream filling a day ahead of time and store it in the refrigerator.

Rose and Mint Infused Fruit Salad (*Salata bil Fakha, Ward, wa Na'na*)

Use whatever fresh fruit is available to make this delicious fruit salad. The fruit should be chopped, tossed to combine, and chilled at least 5 hours before serving to allow the rose and mint flavors to blend properly.

Ingredients:

1 cup cantaloupe, cubed
1 cup honeydew, cubed
1 cup watermelon, cubed
1/4 cup blueberries
1/4 cup kiwi, sliced
1/4 cup sugar
1 teaspoon rose water
4 tablespoons fresh mint, finely chopped
Whipped cream, for garnish, if desired

Preparation:

Combine all fruit in a large salad bowl. Mix sugar, rose water, and mint together in a small bowl. Drizzle sugar mixture over fruit and mix gently to combine.

Cover bowl, and store in refrigerator for a minimum of 5 hours or a maximum of overnight.

Transfer fruit to individual bowls to serve. Garnish with
whipped cream, if desired.
Serves 6 to 8.

Saudi Shortbread Cookies (Ghorayeba)

This is a traditional Saudi Arabian cookie recipe and can be
enjoyed on many special occasions. The cookies are a beautiful
white color and are decorated with a single blanched almond
sliver. The taste of these cookies is enhanced by the refreshing
flavor of cardamom, a spice that is popular throughout the Arabian Peninsula, where a whole pound of ground cardamom can
be purchased for less than ten dollars. These cookies can be frozen for up to one month before serving. Many Arabians bake
them in advance and keep them on hand for unexpected guests.

Ingredients:
Butter, for greasing pans
1 cup organic vegetable shortening
1 cup confectioners' sugar
1 teaspoon ground cardamom
3 cups unbleached, all-purpose flour
1 teaspoon rose water
1 teaspoon orange blossom water
5 ounces blanched (skinless) almonds, slivered

Preparation:
Position racks in the center of the oven. Preheat oven to 350°F.
Grease 2 double air-cell baking sheets* with butter.
Mix shortening and sugar in a large bowl with a wooden
spoon until sugar is completely incorporated. Add the
cardamom, flour, rose water, and orange blossom water. Mix to combine well.
Roll spoonfuls of dough into 1-inch balls and place on baking sheets, leaving 1-inch between each ball. Gently
press an almond sliver into the top of each ball and

---

* To ensure that cookies bake properly and do not brown on the
bottom, use double air-cell baking sheets.

flatten slightly. If dough cracks, mend it by gently smoothing over it with your fingers.

Bake for 12 to 15 minutes, or until tops begin to turn golden. (Cookies should still be white when taken out of oven.) Remove from oven and allow cookies to cool in pan.

These cookies may be stored for up to 1 week at room temperature, or in the freezer for up to 1 month.

Makes about 4 dozen.

Tip: *You can add a few drops of red or green food coloring to the dough to color the cookies, if desired.*

Entertaining Timeline

One month before the tea party or as far in advance as possible:

Invite guests.

Purchase rose-colored table linens, if necessary.

Purchase or mail order dried organic rose buds, rose water, spices, and orange blossom water for recipes.

Purchase an additional bottle of rose water to give to each guest as a favor.

Select soft, romantic instrumental music to play (Arabian *oud* (lute) music is perfect for this occasion).

Make tags with guests' names to tie around roses as place settings.

Make and freeze Saudi Shortbread Cookies.

One week before the tea party:

Confirm number of guests and make grocery list accordingly.

Buy groceries.

Polish silver tea set, if using.

One night before the tea party:

Purchase fresh roses for each place setting.

Make Semolina Squares with Yogurt and store in refrigerator.

Make Cream-filled Phyllo Triangles and store in refrigerator.

Make Rose and Mint Infused Fruit Salad and chill in refrigerator.

Set table with linens and plates.

Day of the tea party:
Remove Saudi Shortbread Cookies from freezer to thaw, and arrange on serving platter.

Arrange Semolina Squares with Yogurt on a serving platter.

Arrange Cream-filled Phyllo Triangles on a serving platter.

Transfer Rose and Mint Infused Salad to individual serving bowls.

Place dried dates and mixed nuts in serving bowls.

Tie nametags around each rose and place one on top of each place setting.

Before guests arrive:
Play music.

Transfer desserts to serving table.

Begin brewing teas as guests arrive.

CHAPTER 4
Palace Spice Brunch

Start your day with the alluring aromas of exotic spices. The intoxicating scents of cloves, roses, wild thyme, sumac, and freshly brewed tea can transform any night owl into a morning person. I was treated to this sort of lavish breakfast buffet during my stay in Saudi Arabia. From the first time I ate these foods, I knew that they would fit perfectly into the American brunch culture.

The theme for this menu is spices. Guests are given bags filled with the *Zataar* Spice Mix as a party favor. Cinnamon sticks are transformed into place card holders. Instead of a traditional flower centerpiece, a spice "potpourri" is placed in the middle of the table. Rich jewel-toned linens—the green of cardamom, ruby of sumac, and pink of rose quartz—adorn the table. Traditional Arabian music, reminiscent of the sounds of an Arabian spice bazaar, sets the mood.

Since most of the menu items for the Palace Spice Brunch can be purchased or made in advance, this is a great menu to serve in the morning. If you have the spices, rose water, *labna*, and date molasses on hand, you can invite your guests on Friday, do your grocery shopping that evening, prepare the food on Saturday, and be ready for brunch on Sunday morning.

Menu

Buffet Items:
Croissants with Wild Thyme (*Khubz bil Zataar*)
Yogurt Cheese with Date Molasses (*Labna bil Dabs al Tamr*)
Date Bread (*Khubz bi Tamr*)
Vermicelli with Strawberries and Cream (*Sharleya bil Frawila wa Halib*)
Spinach Omelet with Pita Chips (*Ejja Mashwiya bil Sabanikh*)

Dried Apricots in Clove Syrup (*Qamr Din Helw bil Qurunfil*)
Dried Figs in Rose Syrup (*Teen Helw bil Ward*)
Assorted Cheese Plate (purchased)

Drinks:
Tea with Milk
Coffee with Cream
Strawberry Cocktail (*Cocktail bil Frawila*)

Tabletop:
Spice Potpourri Centerpiece

Favor:
Zataar Spice Mix (*Zataar*)

Croissants with Wild Thyme (*Khubz bil Zataar*)

Zataar is a kind of wild thyme that grows throughout the Middle East. *Zataar* is also the name of a spice mix that includes wild thyme. These croissants can be made a day ahead of time and be reheated before serving.

Ingredients:

1 (8-ounce) can refrigerated crescent rolls
1/8 cup unsalted butter, melted
1/4 cup Zataar Spice Mix (see page 64)

Preparation:

Preheat oven and open crescent roll can according to package directions. Separate rolls into 8 triangles and place on an ungreased baking sheet. Brush butter on top of each triangle. Sprinkle Zataar Spice Mix on each triangle. Roll up triangle to form crescent roll shape. Brush top of triangle with more butter. Bake 11 to 13 minutes, or until golden brown. Serve warm.

Serves 4 to 6.

Yogurt Cheese with Date Molasses (*Labna bil Dabs al Tamr*)

By itself, yogurt cheese makes the perfect smooth and tangy dip. When topped with date molasses, it is even more special. In rural areas in the Arabian Peninsula, women make yogurt cheese from scratch. In larger towns and cities, it can be found in super-markets. Date molasses is a traditional sweetener throughout the Arabian Peninsula.

Ingredients:
1 cup yogurt cheese (*labna*)*
4 teaspoons date molasses

Preparation:
Spread yogurt cheese onto a small plate. Make a well in the middle of the mound. Pour the date molasses into the well. Serve with warm Croissants with Wild Thyme, toast, and/or pita bread.
Serves 4.

Tip: Date molasses is a great alternative to maple syrup on pancakes and waffles.

Date Bread (*Khubz bí Tamr*)

For this unique date bread, dried dates are pureed and spread throughout the center of the dough as a filling, rather than simply mixed into the batter. This bread can be stored for a few days at room temperature or frozen for up to one month.

Ingredients:
For the batter:
1/3 cup vegetable or canola oil
1 cup sugar
2 cups unbleached, all-purpose flour
1 teaspoon baking soda
Pinch of salt
2 large eggs
For the filling:
2 tablespoons unsalted butter, plus extra for buttering pan

---

*   See "Where to Buy Guide" for purchasing information for *labna* and date molasses.

1/2 pound dried dates, pitted
1 teaspoon orange blossom water

Preparation:
Butter an 8½ x 4½ x 2½-inch loaf pan. Preheat oven to
　　350°F.
Using an electric mixer, or by hand, cream the oil and
　　sugar together in a large bowl. Add flour, baking soda,
　　and salt, and mix well to combine. Add eggs, one at a
　　time, and stir well after each addition.
To make the date puree, combine 2 tablespoons butter,
　　the pitted dates, and orange blossom water in a food
　　processor. Pulse until a smooth paste forms. Add a
　　few teaspoons of water if necessary to achieve the
　　consistency of paste.
Pour half of the batter into the prepared loaf pan. Spoon
　　the date puree onto the batter and smooth with a
　　knife. Pour the rest of the batter on top of the filling
　　and smooth with a spatula. Hit the bottom of the pan
　　on the countertop a few times to release air bubbles.

Bake on center
rack in the oven for
one hour, or until
golden brown. Re-
move from oven
and cool in pan.
Use a knife to
loosen the edges,
and then turn the
pan over to release
the bread. Slice
and serve at room
temperature.
Serves 10.

Date Bread

**Tip: This bread can also be made in muffin tins. Fill each tin
1/3 full of batter, add a tablespoon of filling in the middle,
and pour more batter on top. Bake 20 minutes,
or until golden.**

Vermicelli with Strawberries and Cream
(Shareya bil Frawila wa Halib)

This sweet breakfast dish can also be served as dessert. It is popular with children and adults alike. According to Edward Hamann, culinary instructor and expert on Indian cuisine and culture, in India, a similar dish is made with clarified butter and dates and is served as a dessert during Eid al Fitr. Other berries, raisins, bananas, or mixed nuts can substitute for the strawberries, if preferred.

Ingredients:
2 teaspoons vegetable oil
1 cup vermicelli, broken into small pieces
1/2 cup sugar
1/2 cup warm milk
3/4 cup fresh strawberries, sliced

Preparation:
Heat oil in a medium saucepan over medium heat. Add vermicelli and lightly brown it on all sides. Stir sugar in 2 cups hot water and add to vermicelli. Lower heat to medium low. Simmer, uncovered, 15 to 20 minutes until vermicelli is tender.

Divide vermicelli into bowls. Top each with equal portions of warm milk. Top with strawberries and serve warm.

Makes 4 small bowls.

Tip: If you are making this dish ahead of time, let vermicelli cool after it is finished simmering. Transfer to the refrigerator and store overnight. The next morning, reheat the vermicelli and top with warm milk and strawberries.

Spinach Omelet with Pita Chips
(Ejja Mashwiya bil Sabanikh)

This spinach omelet is a great addition to any brunch buffet. If making the omelet ahead of time, store it in the refrigerator, and fry the pita chips just before serving.

Ingredients:

3/4 cup chopped frozen spinach, thawed
2 tablespoons grated Romano cheese
2 tablespoons bread crumbs
1/4 cup heavy cream
Salt, to taste
Freshly ground pepper, to taste
6 large eggs
2 pita loaves
2 tablespoons olive oil
Sumac,* to taste

Preparation:

Mix spinach, cheese, bread crumbs, and cream together in a
small bowl. Season with salt and pepper. Stir to combine and set aside.

Beat eggs in a medium bowl with a wire whisk until very
foamy. Pour egg mixture into a large, nonstick frying
pan over medium-high heat.

When the eggs begin to set, place a platter larger than the
frying pan over the top of the pan. Remove the pan from
the flame and quickly and gently turn it over so that
the omelet ends up on the platter. Gently slide the omelet back into the skillet, cooked side up. Continue to
cook for 2 to 3 minutes, until almost cooked through.

Add stuffing to the middle of the egg round leaving a 1-inch
border on the top and bottom and a 2-inch border on
the sides. Fold the omelet sides in over the filling so
that they overlap in the middle. Then turn the omelet
over to seal the bottom.

Preheat the broiler. Turn off the flame and cover the omelet
while making pita chips.

Cut each pita loaf into 4 equal portions. Brush olive oil on
top of each piece and sprinkle sumac over the top. Place
on a baking sheet and bake under the broiler for 2 to 4
minutes per side until golden.

---

*   See "Where to Buy Guide" for purchasing information.

Set omelet on the middle of a serving platter and garnish
with pita chips.
Serves 4 to 6.

**Tip: Serve this omelet with soup or salad for a light, yet
satisfying meal.**

Dried Apricots in Clove Syrup
(Qamr Din Helw bil Qurunfil)
I discovered the delight of combining dried apricots and
cloves at a breakfast at the Jeddah Conference Palace in Saudi
Arabia. The apricots used in this recipe may be prepared a day
in advance and stored in the refrigerator.

Ingredients:
1 1/2 cups sugar
1 strip lemon peel
2 teaspoons fresh-squeezed lemon juice
11 ounces dried apricots
1 teaspoon whole cloves, in a cheesecloth spice bag
1 cinnamon stick

Preparation:
To make syrup, combine sugar with 1/2 cup water, lemon
zest, and lemon juice in a medium saucepan over medium heat. Stir to combine and cook until all sugar is
dissolved. Once sugar is dissolved, stop stirring the
syrup and add apricots, whole cloves, and cinnamon
stick. Mix well and simmer 5 minutes, or until apricots
become plump. Remove from heat and cool. Remove cinnamon stick and cloves and transfer to a serving bowl.
Serve at room temperature or cold.
Serves 4 to 6.

**Tip: You can strain the leftover apricots and serve them over
plain yogurt for breakfast with a dash of cinnamon.**

Dried Figs in Rose Syrup
(Teen Helw bil Ward)

Use dried white figs and organic dried rosebuds for this recipe.

Ingredients:
1 1/2 cups sugar
1 strip lemon peel
2 teaspoons lemon juice
18 dried white figs, stems trimmed
1 teaspoon dried organic rosebuds,* in a cheesecloth spice bag
1 teaspoon rose water

Preparation:
To make syrup, combine sugar with 1/2 cup water, lemon zest, and lemon juice in a medium saucepan over medium heat. Stir to combine and cook until all sugar is dissolved. Add figs, rosebuds, and rose water, and stir to combine. Stop stirring, reduce heat to low, and simmer 10 minutes, or until figs become soft and plump. Remove from heat and cool. Remove rosebuds and transfer to a serving bowl. Serve at room temperature or cold.

Serves 4 to 6.

Tip: You can use leftover figs as a topping for vanilla ice cream.

Strawberry Cocktail
(Cocktail bil Frawila)

Both adults and children will love this sweet smoothie.

Ingredients:
2 cups fresh strawberries, trimmed and sliced
1 banana, sliced

---

* See "Where to Buy Guide" for purchasing information.

1 cup cold milk
4 tablespoons honey, or to taste
1/2 cup whipped cream, for garnish
4 teaspoons strawberry syrup, if desired, for garnish

Preparation:

Combine first 4 ingredients in blender. Whip until ingredients are combined and drink is frothy. Taste and adjust honey, if necessary.

Pour drink into 4 clear glasses. Top each with a dollop of whipped cream. Drizzle 1 teaspoon strawberry syrup over the top of each.

Serves 4.

Spice Potpourri Centerpiece

Use this simple mix in place of flowers as a centerpiece for your Palace Spice Brunch.

Ingredients:

1 small package cinnamon sticks
1 small bottle green cardamom pods
1 small bottle whole cloves
1 small bottle fennel seeds
5 dried lemons*
5 dried limes
1 small bag dried organic rosebuds

Preparation:

Slightly crush cinnamon sticks, cardamom pods, cloves, and fennel seeds with a mortar and pestle to release their aromas.

Toss all ingredients together in a medium-sized bowl, tureen, or round vase. Containers or bowls with silver and gold finishes look the best. Place on the center of the table.

---

*   See "Where to Buy Guide" for purchasing information for dried lemons, dried limes, and organic rosebuds.

Zataar Spice Mix
(Zataar)

Zataar is the name of both the wild thyme herb native to the Middle East, and a spice mix in which it is the main ingredient. Whenever purchasing *zataar*, specify whether or not you would like the herb by itself or pre-mixed. Both types can be found in large bags at Middle Eastern import stores. See the "Where to Buy Guide" for mail order information.

Ingredients:
1/4 cup wild thyme (*zataar*)
1/4 cup sumac
1/4 cup white sesame seeds
1/8 cup ground coriander
1/8 cup anise seeds
1 tablespoon sea salt

Preparation:
Whirl ingredients together in a spice blender or food processor to combine. Store in a tightly sealed jar.
Makes 1 cup.

Tip: Zataar Spice Mix is also tasty on pita bread. Brush plain pita bread with olive oil and Zataar Spice Mix and heat it under the broiler for a minute before serving.

To make favors:
Cheesecloth spice sacks or small clear spice jars
1 spool of craft ribbon, in the color of your choice, cut into strips (1 strip for cheesecloth sack or jar)
Small tags with strings to tie around the ribbon (1 for each sack or jar)

Directions:
Fill each cheesecloth spice sack or spice jar with *Zataar* Spice Mix. Tie a ribbon around each bag to seal or around each jar, just under the lid. Write or type a message on each tag, and tie tags to the center of each ribbon.

Entertaining Timeline

Two weeks before the event:
Mail order hard to find items, if necessary.
Invite guests.
Purchase jewel-toned table linens, if necessary.
Purchase cheesecloth spice sacks for favor bags or small clear spice jars.
Select traditional Arabian music to play.
Make Date Bread and store in the freezer.

One week before the event:
Make *Zataar* Spice Mix and spice mix favors.
Make tags with guests' names and place in the center of a cinnamon stick to use as place cards.
Make Spice Potpourri Centerpiece.
Confirm number of guests and make grocery list accordingly.

Two days before the event:
Purchase groceries.

One day before the event:
Make Croissants with Wild Thyme.
Make Yogurt Cheese with Date Molasses.
Make Vermicelli with Strawberries and Cream.
Make Spinach Omelet.
Make Dried Apricots in Clove Syrup.
Make Dried Figs in Rose Syrup.
Set table with linens and plates, place centerpiece in the middle, and place cards and favors at each setting.

Day of the event:
Remove Date Bread from the freezer to thaw.
Make pita chips to go with Spinach Omelet.
Make Strawberry Cocktail.
Transfer all items to serving pieces on buffet table.

Before guests arrive:
Start music.
Begin brewing tea and coffee as guests arrive.

PART 2
SPECIAL CEREMONIES

Henna Night (*Laylat ul Henna*)

Baby-Naming Ceremony (*Aqiqah*)

Yemeni Sabbath Luncheon (*Ghada lil Youm Sebt*)

Ramadan Breakfast (*Sohoor*)

Ramadan Dinner (*Iftaar*)

CHAPTER 5

Henna Night (*Laylat ul Henna*)

Throughout the Arabian Peninsula, a bride to be will traditionally take part in a celebration called henna night on the eve of her wedding. On this night, the bride's female friends and relatives gather to pamper and support her. Henna night is similar to a bridal shower, except the focus is on beauty and grooming, instead of gifts. Food, drinks, music, and dancing are also part of the evening. Henna nights often used to take place at Turkish baths, when they were popular. But nowadays, they usually take place in homes.

The evening takes its name from the henna tattoos that are painted on the bride's body the night before the wedding by a tattoo artist. Typically, the bride is bathed in special blends of oils, flowers, and herbs. Next, she has all of the hair of her body removed. She is perfumed with oils, and tattooed all over with natural henna ink in elaborate patterns.

Henna ink is derived from the henna flower, which grows in the warm Arabian climate. In conservative cultures, only married women are allowed to get henna tattoos, although in most places unmarried girls get the tattoos for purely aesthetic reasons. Natural henna is temporary and washes off after a few weeks of wear. Many believe henna ink has curative properties and it is often applied on ailing areas of the body.

On henna night, while the bride is being groomed, she is showered with love and affection. Older, married women offer her advice on how to achieve a happy marriage. Some of the women attendees may clap and sing about love and marriage, while others dance. The bride is encouraged to eat rich and sweet foods to ensure that she has a rich and sweet life with her husband to be.

Each Arabian culture has put its own stamp on henna night. The types of oils and perfumes used, the type of foods served, and the music played all vary between cultural groups. Some people hold an extended event, while others shorten it to only a few hours before the wedding. I met a few young women who chose not to have one at all because they felt that they were capable of beautifying themselves and didn't want to bother their friends and family.

To me, henna night is one of the most beautiful ceremonies there is. Occasions to get together, bond, and pamper ourselves should be cherished. Whether you are married or single, I encourage you to plan a henna night for your female friends and family members; you won't regret it. Bridal and baby showers, job promotions, and birthdays are all great reasons to host a henna night.

The themes for henna night are gold and fragrance. Essential oils from the Middle East make wonderful favors and presents (see the "Where to Buy Guide"). Gold jewelry is also a traditional gift for the woman who is being honored. The party should be held after dark and last late into the night. A henna artist should be hired to tattoo each of the guests. Henna tattooing kits are now available in the United States (see the "Where to Buy Guide"). They often contain detailed instructions and templates to trace to make the tattoos. Get the whole group involved! Delegate singing, dancing, and food preparations to guests who enjoy those activities.

Menu

Appetizers:
    Rice Croquettes (*Kibbet al Aish*)
    Bread with Meat (*Khubz bi Lahma*)
Soup:
    Cream of Shrimp Soup (*Hasaa bil Jamberi*)
Salads:
    Bulgur, Tomato, and Cucumber Salad (*Tabbouli*)
    Fattoush Salad (*Salata Fattoush*)
Main Courses:
    Eggplant *Fattah* (*Fattah Batinjan*)
    Citrus and Tomato Glazed Chicken Breasts (*Sadriyat Al Dajaj*)
    Lamb *Kabsah* with Cracked Wheat (*Kabsah bil Jarrish*)
Drink:
    Pink Lady Cocktail (*Cocktail Amra'a Warda*)

Desserts:
> Dried Dates (purchased)
> Melon *K'nafeh* (*K'nafeh Bil Shamman*)
> Date Dome Cookies (*Ma'moul*)
> Candied Almonds (purchased)

Rice Croquettes (*Kibbet al Aish*)

Rice croquettes make a great accompaniment to soup and salad.

Ingredients:
1 1/2 cups short grain rice, rinsed
1 medium potato, peeled and diced
1 teaspoon salt, plus more to taste
1 teaspoon turmeric
1 teaspoon cinnamon
Freshly ground pepper, to taste
2 tablespoons tomato paste
4 cups plus 1 tablespoon corn oil, divided
1 onion, diced
1/2 pound ground beef or lamb
1 teaspoon Saudi Spice Mix (see page 3)
1/4 cup fresh cilantro, chopped

Preparation:
Place rice and potato in a large saucepan and cover with boiling water. Add salt to taste, turmeric, cinnamon, freshly ground pepper, and tomato paste. Bring to a boil over high heat. Reduce heat to medium and boil for 20 to 30 minutes until potatoes begin to become tender. Mash with a potato masher being sure everything is mixed well. Stir to incorporate all ingredients. Set aside and cool to room temperature. (The rice-potato mixture can be made a day ahead and kept in the refrigerator overnight.)

Heat 1 tablespoon corn oil in a large skillet over medium heat. Brown onion and meat together and add Saudi Spice Mix, 1 teaspoon salt, and cilantro. Stir to combine. Once meat is browned, remove from heat and allow to cool. Place mixture in a bowl. (This mixture can be made a day ahead and kept in the refrigerator overnight.)

Place water in a small bowl. Set water bowl next to rice-potato mixture and meat mixture on the counter. Dip fingers in water, and roll pieces of the rice and potato mixture into 3-inch balls. Continue to wet both hands and the croquettes as you work to prevent sticking. Flatten each ball into a disk and fill each with 1/2 teaspoon of meat mixture. Wrap rice and potato mixture around filling to enclose. Roll into an egg shape and set on a large platter. Continue stuffing croquettes until all ingredients are used.

Heat the remaining 4 cups of oil in a large frying pan. When oil is hot, carefully lower rice croquettes into the pan using a slotted spoon. Fill the pan with remaining croquettes, being careful not to crowd pan. Fry for 4 to 5 minutes on each side until golden. Remove from oil with slotted spoon and sprinkle with more salt, if desired. Serve warm.

Makes approximately 2 dozen. Serves 8 to 10.

Tip: You can make the rice and filling a day ahead of time, and then assemble and fry them just before serving.

Bread with Meat (Khubz bi Lahma)

Bread with Meat is an Arabian classic. Nowadays, most women buy bread dough from the baker or pizza dough from a pizza shop to make Bread with Meat. Recently, people have begun using prepared biscuits, found in the dairy case, for making this dish. Bread with Meat can be served with Cucumber and Yogurt Salad (see page 33) and Mixed Salad (see page 32) for a quick lunch or dinner.

Ingredients:
1/2 pound ground beef
1 onion, finely chopped
Salt, to taste
1 teaspoon Saudi Spice Mix (see page 3)
4 tablespoons tahini (sesame paste)
1 teaspoon vinegar

Dash of chili powder
1 tablespoon corn oil
1 (16-ounce) can prepared biscuits
1/4 cup flour, for dusting
4 tablespoons pine nuts

Preparation:
Preheat oven to 350°F.

To make meat filling, brown ground beef and onion together in a large frying pan over medium heat. Season with salt and Saudi Spice Mix. Once meat is browned, set aside. Allow meat to cool and stir in tahini, vinegar, and chili powder.

Grease two baking sheets with corn oil or line with parchment paper or silicone mats.

Remove biscuits from package. Dust a work surface and rolling pin with flour. Roll biscuits out into 5-inch rounds. Place 4 on each baking sheet. Evenly spread filling on top of each one leaving a 1/4-inch border around edges. Sprinkle the tops of each evenly with pine nuts. Bake for 11 to 15 minutes until bread is golden.

Serve warm or cool. Or, wrap in plastic wrap and freeze for up to 1 month.

Makes 8 pieces. Serves 4.

Tip: You can make this recipe the night before and store the rounds in the refrigerator before baking. When you're ready for dinner the next day just pop them in the oven and make the Cucumber and Yogurt and Mixed salads. You'll have dinner ready in less time than it takes to order a pizza.

Cream of Shrimp Soup (*Hasaa bil Jamberi*)
This soup is quick enough to make on a busy weeknight but special enough to serve to guests.

Ingredients:
2 tablespoons olive oil
2 carrots, diced
2 celery stalks, diced

2 pounds shrimp, cleaned, peeled, and deveined*
4 tablespoons unsalted butter
4 tablespoons flour
Dash of cayenne pepper
4 cups whole milk
Salt, to taste
Freshly ground pepper, to taste
2 cups frozen corn, thawed
2 tablespoons chopped parsley

Preparation:

Heat olive oil in a large frying pan over medium heat. Add carrots and celery and sauté until soft, about 5 minutes. Add shrimp and cook 3 to 5 minutes per side until cooked through. Remove from heat.

In a large saucepan melt butter over medium heat. Whisk in flour until incorporated. Allow mixture to cook 2 to 3 minutes until golden brown. Stir in cayenne pepper. Slowly add milk, whisking to make a sauce. Bring to a boil over high heat for 2 minutes, whisking constantly. Reduce to low and cook until sauce thickens, about 5 minutes, still whisking constantly. Season with salt and freshly ground pepper.

Add shrimp and vegetables and corn to the sauce and cook for two minutes. Taste and adjust seasonings if necessary. Remove from heat and add parsley. Serve warm.

Serves 4 to 6.

Bulgur, Tomato, and Cucumber Salad (Tabbouli)

Tabbouli originated in Lebanon, where it is known as *tabouleh*. It is a nutritious lunch or picnic item that is often included in everyday family meals. The cracked wheat provides fiber, and the herbs are packed with vitamins and minerals.

---

* To devein a shrimp, hold it with its back facing upward. Make a split down the length of the spine with a paring knife and remove the black thread.

Cucumbers level the body temperature in warmer climates, are rich in potassium, and are said to prevent eczema, fevers, psoriasis, and fluid retention. Tomatoes contain the powerful antioxidant lycopene, known to fight cancer.

Ingredients:

1 cup bulgur wheat #1*
1/4 cup extra-virgin olive oil (first cold press if possible)
Juice of 1 lemon
Juice of 1 lime
Salt, to taste
Freshly ground pepper, to taste
4 small cucumbers, diced
4 roma tomatoes, diced
1 small onion, grated
3/4 cup fresh parsley, chopped
1/4 cup fresh mint, chopped
1 head of romaine lettuce, leaves cleaned and rinsed

Preparation:

Pour bulgur into a large bowl. Cover it with enough water to cover plus 2 inches. Let stand for 1 hour.

Mix bulgur with olive oil, lemon juice, and lime juice.† Add salt and pepper to taste. Add diced vegetables and chopped herbs. Stir. Taste and adjust seasonings if necessary.

Refrigerate for 1 hour or up to 12 hours. Serve with large whole romaine leaves.

Serves 6 to 8.

Tip: Eat tabbouli as the Lebanese do, by wrapping it in romaine lettuce leaves instead of pita bread.

---

* See "Where to Buy Guide" for purchasing information.

† To make *tabbouli* more than one day in advance, simply omit the citrus juices while preparing the salad. Refrigerate the salad overnight or for a few days, and add the lemon and lime juice just before serving.

Fattoush Salad (Salata Fattoush)

Fattoush Salad is a delicious cucumber and tomato salad tossed with crunchy toasted pita pieces and dressed with pomegranate molasses dressing. It's a great way to use leftover pita bread.

Ingredients:

1 cucumber, diced
4 tomatoes, chopped finely
1 red onion, thinly sliced
1 pita, cut into 12 pieces
1/2 cup extra-virgin olive oil (first cold press if possible), divided
4 teaspoons sumac[*]
2 tablespoons pomegranate molasses
Juice of 1 lemon
Salt, to taste
Freshly ground pepper, to taste

Preparation:

Preheat broiler.
Combine cucumber, tomatoes, and red onion in a large salad bowl.
Brush pita pieces with 2 tablespoons olive oil and sprinkle with sumac. Place under broiler and toast for 2 to 4 minutes, until golden on both sides. Remove from oven and set aside to cool.
Mix remaining olive oil, pomegranate molasses, lemon juice, salt, and pepper in a medium bowl. Whisk vigorously to form a smooth dressing. Add pita chips to salad and toss to combine. Pour dressing over salad and toss again to combine. Serve immediately.
Serves 4 to 6.

Tip: Toss leftover morsels of lamb meat with Fattoush *Salad* **for a quick lunch or dinner.**

---

[*]   See "Where to Buy Guide" for purchasing information for sumac and pomegranate molasses.

Eggplant *Fattah* (*Fattah Batínjan*)

The word *fattah* is derived from *fattat*, which means "fully grown girl" in Arabic. When *fattah* is used to describe a food, it denotes one ingredient, such as eggplant, chicken, lamb, or chickpeas, that has "grown" by layering other ingredients with it.

This recipe originated in Lebanon. The name of Lebanon itself came from the word *labna*, which means yogurt cheese, because it is a specialty of the region. This recipe is topped with creamy *labna*.

Ingredients:
1 cup vegetable or canola oil, for frying
1 medium eggplant, sliced into 1/4-inch-thick rounds
1 teaspoon sumac,* plus more to taste
Salt, to taste
Freshly ground pepper, to taste
3 pita breads, cut into 1-inch pieces
1 cup cooked or canned chickpeas, drained
2 garlic cloves, minced
2 cups yogurt cheese (*labna*)
1/4 cup pine nuts

Preparation:
Preheat oven to 350°F.

Heat oil in a large saucepan over medium heat. Fry egg-plant until golden on each side, turning once. Remove from oil with a slotted spoon and drain on dishes lined with paper towels. Sprinkle with 1 teaspoon sumac, salt, and pepper.

Fry bread pieces in the same oil until golden. Remove with a slotted spoon onto dishes lined with paper towels.

Line a baking casserole with 1/3 of the fried bread. Top with 1/2 of fried eggplant and chickpeas. Top with 1/3 of bread pieces. Repeat with remaining eggplant and chickpeas. Season with sumac, salt, and pepper. Top with remaining bread.

---

* See "Where to Buy Guide" for purchasing information for sumac and *labna*.

Mix garlic with yogurt cheese. Spoon yogurt cheese on top
of fattah. Sprinkle pine nuts and more sumac on top of
the yogurt cheese.
Bake for 15 to 20 minutes, or until yogurt cheese is melted
and pine nuts begin to turn color.
Serves 4 to 6.

Citrus and Tomato Glazed Chicken Breasts (Sadriyat Al Dajaj)

This quick and easy entrée is special enough to serve on
festive occasions, yet fast enough to make on a busy weeknight.
Any chicken parts could be used instead of chicken breasts.

Ingredients:
2 tablespoons corn oil
1 pound chicken breasts, sliced in half widthwise
1 medium yellow onion, sliced
1 garlic clove, minced
2 teaspoons Saudi Spice Mix (see page 3)
1/2 cup tomatoes, chopped
1 tablespoon tomato paste
3/4 cup chicken stock
Juice of 1 lemon
Juice of 1 orange

Preparation:
Heat oil in a large frying pan over medium-high heat. Add
chicken and brown on all sides. Remove chicken from
pan, place on a plate, and set aside.
Add onion to pan and sauté until translucent. Add garlic and
spice mix and cook for one minute, stirring. Return chicken
to the pan. Add tomatoes, tomato paste, chicken stock,
and lemon and orange juice. Increase heat to high and
bring to a boil. Reduce heat to low and cook, covered,
for 30 minutes, or until chicken is cooked through.
Serves 4.

**Tip: Serve chicken with white rice and a green leafy
vegetable for a complete meal.**

Lamb Kabsah with Cracked Wheat
(Kabsah bil Jarrish)

Kabsah is a traditional dish from Saudi Arabia in which morsels of beef, chicken, or lamb are slowly simmered with stock and spices. Many versions contain rice. This version, however, contains *jarrish*, a kind of cracked wheat that is popular in the Arabian Peninsula.

Ingredients:

4 teaspoons clarified butter (ghee), divided
2 medium onions, cut into thin strips
1/2 cup tomatoes, chopped
3 teaspoons Saudi Spice Mix (see page 3)
1 tablespoon tomato paste
5 cups chicken stock
2 pounds boneless lamb shoulder, cubed
2 cups cracked wheat*
1/4 cup almonds, slivered
1/4 cup raisins
1/4 cup pine nuts

Preparation:

Heat 3 teaspoons clarified butter in a large saucepan over medium heat. Add onions and sauté until translucent, about 5 minutes. Add chopped tomatoes, spice mix, tomato paste, and stock. Stir well and add meat to the pot. Increase the heat to high and bring to a boil. Turn the heat down to low, cover, and simmer for 1 1/2 hours.

Remove lid, stir, taste, and adjust the seasonings if necessary. Add the cracked wheat to the pot and stir. Cover and continue to cook for 30 to 45 minutes over low heat until wheat is tender.

Melt remaining teaspoon of clarified butter in a small frying pan over medium heat. Add almonds, raisins, and pine nuts and fry for 1 to 2 minutes until nuts begin to turn color and raisins puff up.

---

* See "Where to Buy Guide" for purchasing information.

When *kabsah* is finished cooking, turn it out onto a large serving
platter with high edges. Garnish with nuts and raisins.
Serves 4 to 6.

Pink Lady Cocktail (*Cocktail Amra'a Warda*)

This whimsical drink includes guava juice with milk and
grenadine. Serve in crystal glasses to show off its pink color.

Ingredients:
4 cups cold guava juice (white or pink)
4 cups cold milk
4 teaspoons grenadine

Preparation:
Place all ingredients in a mixer and whip until blended. Pour
into glasses and serve immediately or store in a pitcher
in the refrigerator.
Serves 6 to 8.

Melon K'nafeh (*K'nafeh Bil Shammam*)

Melon *K'nafeh* is unique to the Arabian Gulf. The flavors of
melon and cardamom provide a cool and refreshing contrast to
the butter and syrup soaked *kataifi* strands. Keep in mind that
kataifi needs to be thawed according to package instructions
before it is used.

Ingredients:
For the syrup:
2 cups sugar
1 cup water
1 teaspoon lemon juice
1 teaspoon orange blossom water
1 teaspoon rose water
For the k'nafeh:
1 cup unsalted butter, melted
1 package *kataifi* strands*

---

*   See "Where to Buy Guide" for purchasing information.

1 ripe honeydew, cut into thin slices
2 teaspoons ground cardamom
2 teaspoons sugar
1/4 cup pistachios, finely chopped, for garnish

Preparation:

To make the syrup, combine sugar, water, and lemon juice in a medium saucepan. Bring to a boil over medium heat, stirring until sugar dissolves. Once sugar is dissolved, stop stirring and reduce heat to low. Allow to simmer 10 to 15 minutes, until syrup is thick. Remove from heat, stir in orange blossom and rose water, and allow to cool.

Preheat oven to 350°F. Line an 8-inch round baking pan with parchment paper.

Place butter in a large deep bowl. Remove *kataifi* from package and hold over bowl. Break into small pieces with your fingers and drop into butter. Mix well to evenly coat all strands with butter. Break up any large pieces (each piece should be approximately an inch or less).

Remove half of the strands and press them into the base of the prepared baking pan to cover. Arrange melon slices evenly over the strands. Mix cardamom and sugar together and sprinkle over the melon. Press remaining *kataifi* strands over the melon. Press down firmly to seal.

Bake for 50 to 60 minutes, or until golden. Pour syrup evenly over *k'nafeh*.

Turn *k'nafeh* out onto a plate. Garnish with pistachios. Serve at room temperature, in wedges.

Store remaining *k'nafeh* in refrigerator, covered with plastic for up to 1 day.

Serves 6 to 8.

Tip: *Prepare Melon K'nafeh up to the point of baking a day in advance and refrigerate. Bake and cover with syrup before serving.*

Date Dome Cookies (Ma'moul)

These scrumptious cookies are to Saudi Arabians what chocolate chip cookies are to Americans. They can be purchased everywhere, from bakeries to grocery stores, which sell pre-boxed varieties. Their fillings range from date and apple to pistachio and walnut. By far, the date cookies are the most coveted. Originally, *ma'moul* were called *aroosa*, which means bride, because they were dusted with white powdered sugar and played an important role in bridal ceremonies.

Ma'moul are made with special wooden (and nowadays plastic) molds called *qaleb*. The molds are engraved with various designs to decorate the cookies in intricate patterns. Refer to the "Where to Buy Guide" for purchasing information or simply shape the cookies into balls. For best results, use double air-cell or stone cookie sheets to prevent the cookies from burning on the bottom.

Ingredients:

For the date filling:
1/2 pound dried dates, pitted
2 tablespoons butter
1 teaspoon orange blossom water
For the cookie dough:
1 cup unsalted butter, at room temperature
1 1/2 cups sugar
2 teaspoons fresh orange or lemon juice
1 teaspoon orange blossom water
1 large egg

1/2 teaspoon *mahlab**
3 cups unbleached, all-purpose flour
1 cup fine-grade semolina
1/2 teaspoon salt
Confectioners' sugar, for sprinkling

Preparation:

Preheat oven to 350°F. Position racks in the middle of the oven. Line two double air-cell or stone cookie sheets with silicone liners or parchment paper.

To prepare date filling, combine the filling ingredients in a food processor. Pulse until filling reaches a paste-like consistency. Set aside.

Combine butter and sugar in a large bowl. Cream until light yellow in color, about 3 to 5 minutes. Add orange or lemon juice and orange blossom water and mix well. Add egg and *mahlab* and stir to incorporate. Mix flour, semolina, and salt in a separate large bowl. Slowly add flour mixture to the butter mixture. Mix the dough until it becomes smooth and shape it into a ball.

To assemble the *ma'moul*, determine which size mold you are using. For a large mold, shape dough into 2-inch balls. For a small mold, shape dough into 1 1/2-inch balls. Flatten balls and place 1 teaspoon date mixture into the center of each circle. Stretch the dough to cover filling and roll back into a ball. Place balls, one at a time, in the mold. Push dough into the mold until it is level with the mold and smooth it out to fill the entire space. To unmold the cookie, hold the stick of the mold and tap its neck, with the cookie facing away from you, onto a hard surface.

Place cookies design side up onto the cookie sheet. Cookies may be placed 1/2 inch apart from one another because they do not spread.

---

*   See "Where to Buy Guide" for purchasing information for *mahlab* and semolina.

Bake about 20 minutes. Do not let tops of cookies turn color. Remove from the oven and top with sifted confectioners' sugar. Allow cookies to cool in sheets on wire racks. *Makes 30 to 40 cookies.*

Tip: These cookies can be frozen for up to a month in an airtight container between sheets of wax paper.

Entertaining Timeline

One month to two weeks before the event:
Invite guests.
Mail order hard to find items, if necessary.
Purchase essential oils for favors.
Purchase gift for the woman of honor.
Hire henna artist to give tattoos or buy a henna tattooing kit. Arrange for the henna artist to arrive 2 hours after the party begins so guests have time to eat before getting tattoos. Keep in mind that henna tattoos take at least 1 hour to dry completely.
Purchase gold or white table linens, if necessary.
Purchase candied almonds.
Select traditional Arabian music to play.
Make Bread with Meat and store in freezer.
Make Date Dome Cookies and store in the freezer.

One week before the event:
Confirm number of guests and make grocery list accordingly.

Three days before the event:
Buy groceries.

One day before the event:
Make Rice Croquettes and refrigerate.
Make Cream of Shrimp Soup and refrigerate.
Make Citrus and Tomato Glazed Chicken Breasts and refrigerate.
Make Melon *K'nafeh* and refrigerate.
Set up buffet table with linens.

Day of the event:

Make Bulgur, Tomato, and Cucumber Salad and *Fattoush* Salad and store at room temperature.

Remove Bread with Meat and Date Dome Cookies from freezer to thaw.

Three to four hours before event:

Make Lamb *Kabsah* with Cracked Wheat.

Make Eggplant *Fattah*.

Arrange dates, candied almonds, and desserts on serving platters.

Make and pour Pink Lady Cocktail into a serving pitcher or glasses.

Reheat refrigerated items.

Begin playing music as guests arrive.

CHAPTER 6
Baby-Naming Ceremony (Aqiqah)

Aqiqahs, or baby-naming ceremonies, are performed throughout the Muslim world. They usually take place 7 to 40 days after a baby is born and are meant to welcome the baby into the world and to introduce it to important Islamic rituals. Islamic tradition dictates that a baby's name represent an aspect of the birth process and the baby's character—thus, the babies of Muslim families are not named until after they are born, during the *aqiqah*.

Charity is an important ritual of the naming ceremony. The baby's head is shaved, its hair is weighed, and the weight of its hair is to be distributed to the needy as charity in the form of silver, gold, and meat. Many families sacrifice sheep or goats during the *aqiqah* and give the meat to the poor to show their appreciation to Allah for having been blessed with a child.

Several religious and cultural traditions are part of the *aqiqah*. Traditionally, male babies were circumcised during the ceremony. Recipes symbolizing sweetness, wealth, fertility, and longevity are served. Imams (Islamic prayer leaders) lead guests in prayers to bless the baby. Gifts are given to the baby's parents as well.

Often in the Arabian Peninsula whole communities take part in *aqiqahs*. In America, however, individual families must interpret the customs by themselves and organize *aqiqahs* on their own. Some families choose to wait a long time after a baby's birth before holding the *aqiqah* so that they have more time to plan.

U.S. law requires that baby names be chosen and male babies be circumcised in the hospital. Some families in America name their babies for legal reasons but don't reveal the names to the public until the *aqiqah*. Other families perform the ritual charity, prayers, and blessings while forgoing the elaborate parties.

Many aspects of the *aqiqah* can be easily integrated into American baby showers as well as Judaic and Christian birth ceremonies. Holding a ceremony after a baby is born enables families to welcome the baby and allows relatives an opportunity to get involved in a baby's life early on. Giving charity and remembering the less fortunate at celebrations is also a wonderful tradition for anyone to start.

The color theme for this party is white to symbolize the innocence and purity of the baby and wheat to symbolize fertility. Some of the recipes chosen for this menu either contain wheat or have the word "mother" or "father" in their name. The overall mood of the party is festive and thankful. All menu items are easy to prepare and can be made in advance.

Menu

Appetizers:
Stuffed Grape Leaves (*Wara' Aghnib*)
Eggplant Puree (*Baba Ghanouj*)
Pita Bread (purchased)
Beef and Cilantro *Kofta* (*Koftat Lahma bil Qusbara*)
Cracked Wheat with Yogurt (*Jarrish bil Laban*)

Soup:
Lamb and Lavash Soup (*Tharid*)

Main Course:
Chicken Stuffed with Rice and Meat (*Dajaj Mashwy*)

Drink:
Mint Tea (*Shai bil Na'na*)

Dessert:
Ali's Mother's Bread Pudding (*Om'Ali*)

Favor:
Jordan Almonds (purchased)

Stuffed Grape Leaves (*Wara' Aghnib*)

Stuffed Grape Leaves can be served as an appetizer, side dish, or buffet item. They can be served with varying amounts of filling. In Saudi Arabia, I ate delicious, plump versions stuffed with rice, herbs, and tomatoes.

Ingredients:
1 (8-ounce) jar preserved vine leaves
1/3 cup fresh dill
1/3 cup fresh parsley
1/3 cup fresh mint
1 cup short grain rice, rinsed
1 cup canned chopped tomatoes, juices drained, divided
1 medium onion, grated
1/4 cup extra-virgin olive oil
Salt, to taste
Freshly ground pepper, to taste
Dash of chili powder
2 lemons, sliced

Preparation:
Pull vine leaves gently apart. Place in a large bowl. Soak in
    boiling water to cover for 10 minutes.
Finely chop dill, parsley, and mint.
In a medium bowl, mix rice, herbs, 3/4 cup tomatoes, onion,
    olive oil, salt, pepper, and chili powder.
Drain grape leaves and place on a work surface, vein side
    up. Cut excess stem from the bottom of each leaf. Place
    one tablespoon of rice mixture in the middle of a leaf.
    Shape the filling to the width of a pencil across the cen-
    ter of each leaf. Roll up, starting at the bottom, tucking
    in the sides of the leaf as you go to make an envelope.
    Try to roll loose enough so that the leaf will not burst
    as the rice cooks and expands inside. Continue with
    the remaining leaves.
Stack rolls seam side down in a heavy saucepan that is
    large enough to accommodate all of the rolls snugly
    in one layer. Place a dish upside down on top of leaves
    to keep them submerged in water. Pour boiling wa-
    ter over rolls until they are almost, but not completely,
    covered. Add the remaining 1/4 cup tomatoes and salt
    and pepper to pan. Cover pot and simmer on low heat
    until rice is fully cooked and leaves are tender, about
    1 to 1 1/2 hours.

Test leaves by cutting one in half and sampling the rice. Rice should be fully cooked when water has been absorbed. If liquid disappears before rice is fully cooked, add more boiling water 1/2 cup at a time until the rice is done.

Serve with lemon slices. May be served warm, at room temperature, or cold.

Serves 4 to 6. Makes 25 to 30.

Tip: Assemble Stuffed Grape Leaves a day in advance and place in saucepan. Cook the following day.

Eggplant Puree (Baba Ghanouj)

This Arabian classic is much simpler to prepare at home than many people realize. When purchasing eggplants, look for those that are shiny, bright, and free of bruises. Since this dish is not heated, it's perfect for buffets and picnics. Using first cold press extra-virgin olive oil or unfiltered olive oil will improve the taste a great deal.

Ingredients:

2 (8- to 9-inch-long) eggplants
2 tablespoons tahini (sesame paste)
Salt, to taste
Juice of 1 lemon
Extra-virgin olive oil, as needed
Dash of sumac,* for garnish

Preparation:

Preheat broiler. Prick eggplants with a fork and place on a baking sheet. Broil 15 to 20 minutes, turning once, until eggplants are blistered. Cool. Peel and remove skin. Place pulp in a colander to drain. Press down with a fork until all liquid is removed.

Place eggplant pulp in a medium bowl. With a fork, stir in tahini, salt, and lemon juice. Add olive oil, a tablespoon at a time, until the texture of the puree

---

* See "Where to Buy Guide" for purchasing information.

resembles crunchy peanut butter. The amount of olive oil needed will depend on the water content and size of the eggplants used. You should still be able to see eggplant pieces in the puree; it should not be perfectly smooth.

Make a small well in the center of the puree and fill with olive oil. Season with sumac.

Serve at room temperature with pita bread or crudités.

Serves 4.

Tip: Roast eggplants a day ahead and assemble Eggplant Puree at the last minute.

Beef and Cilantro Kofta (Koftat Lahma bil Qusbara)

These delicious beef fritters are filled with spices and fresh cilantro. Parsley can be used in place of the cilantro, if you prefer. Also, the fritters can be grilled or baked instead of fried.

Ingredients:
2 pounds lean ground beef, rinsed and drained well
1/4 cup fresh cilantro, stems removed
1 large onion, roughly chopped
2 teaspoons Saudi Spice Mix (see page 3)
Corn oil, for frying
Salt, to taste

Preparation:
Mix ground beef, cilantro, onion, and Saudi Spice Mix in a food processor or in a large bowl with a wooden spoon to form a paste. Shape meat mixture into 3-inch finger shapes.

Pour oil 1 inch deep into a large, shallow frying pan over medium-high heat. When oil is hot (about 300°F), lower *kofta* carefully into pan. Add more *kofta*, leaving an inch between each one. Fry for approximately 5 minutes on each side, or until golden brown and cooked through. Remove with slotted spoon onto a platter lined with paper towels.

Season with salt and serve warm, with lime wedges and
rice.

Serves 4 to 6.

Cracked Wheat with Yogurt (*Jarrish bil Laban*)

Cracked Wheat with Yogurt is the Arabian version of grits
with butter. I first sampled *jarrish* at the conference palace in
Jeddah, Saudi Arabia. I was reluctant to try it because its name
and appearance do not come close to describing its soothing, rich
flavor. This is a satisfying dish, made by simmering cracked
wheat, yogurt, and clarified butter together for 3 hours. Keep in
mind that the cooking time is not active time, meaning this dish
is easy to make. You just mix the ingredients together, put it on
the stove, and forget about it until it's ready to serve.

Ingredients:
2 cups plain yogurt, drained
1 tablespoon salt
1/2 cup clarified butter (ghee)
2 chili peppers, diced
2 tablespoons coriander
2 cups cracked wheat, rinsed and drained

Preparation:
Place yogurt and salt in a medium saucepan over low heat.
Stir until mixture begins to boil.

Mix clarified butter, chili peppers, and coriander together
and add to yogurt mixture. Stir well to combine and
add cracked wheat. Mix well again. Cover the pan and
reduce heat to the lowest setting possible. Simmer for
3 hours, or until wheat is tender.

Press wheat mixture into an 8-inch round baking pan and
smooth the top with a spatula. Push the rim of a small
glass in the center of the mixture to make a hole. Place
a plate over the top of the pan, and turn upside down to
release the wheat mixture onto the plate. Cut the wheat
mixture into slices and serve warm.

Serves 6.

Lamb and Lavash Soup (*Tharid*)

This is a version of what is said to have been the Prophet Muhammad's favorite dish. His wife, Aisha, garnished the *tharid* with a mixture of bran flour and honey called *talbina.* Many different recipes for this dish exist. Some of them, however, contain ingredients, such as tomatoes, potatoes, and spices, that were not available in the seventh century in Mecca. This version tastes a bit like French onion soup with the addition of lamb meat.

Ingredients:

2 tablespoons clarified butter (ghee), divided
1 onion, diced
2 pounds boneless lamb shoulder, cubed
1 teaspoon ground cumin
1 teaspoon ground ginger
1 cinnamon stick
Salt, to taste
Freshly ground pepper, to taste
8 cloves garlic, minced
2 cups chicken or beef broth
4 (6-inch) squares of lavash or pita bread, cut into 2- to 3-inch pieces
4 tablespoons fresh parsley, chopped

Preparation:

Heat 1 tablespoon clarified butter in a large saucepan over medium heat. Add onion and sauté until lightly golden. Then add meat, stir, and brown on all sides. Add cumin, ginger, cinnamon stick, salt, pepper, and garlic. Mix well to combine. Add broth and stir well. Increase heat to high and bring to a boil, uncovered. Reduce heat to low, stir, and cover. Simmer for 1 1/2 hours. When soup is ready, turn off heat.

Preheat broiler and place bread pieces on a baking sheet. Place baking sheet under broiler and toast bread for 1 to 2 minutes on each side, until golden.

With a slotted spoon, remove lamb meat from broth and place on top of toasted bread. Brush lamb with remaining 1 tablespoon clarified butter and place under broiler for 1 minute.

Taste broth and adjust seasonings if necessary. Remove cinnamon stick.

Divide bread and lamb into 4 soup bowls or place in a tureen. Pour broth over bread and lamb. Garnish with parsley and serve hot.

Serves 4.

Chicken Stuffed with Rice and Meat (Dajaj Mashwy)

In this recipe, the classic stuffed chicken gets a flavor boost from rice, meat, spices, raisins, almonds, and a tomato puree. I like to add chickpeas to the tomato topping because the chickpeas' flavor reminds me of the roasted chickpeas that can be bought at street-side stands all over the Middle East.

Ingredients:
3 tablespoons corn oil, divided
1/4 pound ground beef or lamb
1 small onion, diced
Salt, to taste
Freshly ground pepper, to taste
1 cup cooked *Khaleeji* White Rice (see page 160) or any left over rice
1/8 cup slivered almonds
1/8 cup raisins
1 teaspoon Saudi Spice Mix (see page 3)
1 whole chicken, cleaned and rinsed well
1 cup tomato puree
1 cup cooked chickpeas

Preparation:
Preheat oven to 425°F.

Heat 1 tablespoon corn oil in a large frying pan over medium heat. Add meat and onion and cook until meat is browned. Season with salt and freshly ground pepper. Pour into a large bowl and stir in rice, almonds, raisins, and Saudi Spice Mix.

Grease a 9x13-inch baking pan or a roasting pan with a lid with remaining 2 tablespoons corn oil. Place chicken in pan and turn to coat with oil. Stuff chicken with meat mixture. Place chicken breastside up in pan. Pour tomato puree over chicken. Scatter chickpeas around the base of the pan and mix with tomato puree. Season with salt and freshly ground pepper.

Cover with aluminum foil or lid and bake for 1 to 1 1/2 hours, or until chicken is done. (Chicken is done when clear juices run from the thickest part of the thigh after it is pierced with a fork.)

Serves 4.

Tip: Use leftover meat from Bread with Meat (see page 71) for a fast stuffing. Or, cook the meat the night before.

Mint Tea (*Shai bil Na'na*)

This is a calming tea that promotes digestion and clears the nasal passages.

Ingredients:

1/2 cup fresh mint or 2 tablespoons dried mint
2 cups water
Sugar, to taste

Preparation:

If using fresh mint, wash it thoroughly. Place mint in a teapot or medium saucepan. Cover with water and bring to a medium boil over high heat. Take the pot off of heat and steep for 5 minutes. Strain and pour into tea cups. Add sugar. Serve warm.

Serves 2.

Ali's Mother's Bread Pudding (*Om'Ali*)

I ate the Arabian version of this Egyptian classic at the guest palace in Mecca, which overlooks the courtyard of the Great Mosque. It was served in a huge, free-standing chaffing dish with a dome lid at the end of an already enormous dessert buffet. This version tastes more like a traditional American bread pudding with coconut, apricots, and pistachios added to it than like the more creamy Egyptian version. It's sweet and simple and can be prepared in moments. This is a great recipe to make when you need to take a dish to an event.

Ingredients:
1 tablespoon butter, for greasing pan
1 day-old classic French baguette, cut into 1-inch cubes (5 cups total)
1/2 cup shredded coconut
1/2 cup dried apricots
1/2 cup pistachios, shelled
1/2 cup plus 1 tablespoon sugar, divided
1 teaspoon orange blossom water
2 cups whole milk
1 teaspoon vanilla
2 large egg yolks, lightly beaten
1 teaspoon rose water
1 cup heavy cream
Vanilla ice cream, for serving, if desired

Preparation:
Butter a 9x13-inch or 10-inch oval baking dish. Preheat oven to 350°F.

Place bread chunks in the bottom of the baking dish. Mix coconut and dried apricots together and scatter over the bread.

In a food processor, combine pistachios with 1 tablespoon sugar and orange blossom water. Pulse until pistachios are coarsely ground. Sprinkle mixture on top of bread.

In a medium saucepan over medium heat, heat milk, vanilla, and 1/2 cup sugar until just boiling. Add 1 tablespoon of hot milk to beaten eggs. Slowly pour egg mixture into milk mixture, and stir vigorously for 2 minutes. Take milk off heat, stir in rosewater, and pour evenly over bread in baking dish.

Pour cream evenly over ingredients in the dish.

Bake, uncovered, for 25 to 30 minutes or until bread is golden and liquid has thickened. Serve warm or at room temperature with vanilla ice cream, if desired.

Serves 6 to 8.

Tip: Try serving Om' Ali *for breakfast on special occasions by making it the night before, refrigerating it, and reheating it in the morning.*

Entertaining Timeline

One month before the event:

Send invitations to family and friends.

Confirm number of guests and make grocery list accordingly.

Mail order hard to find items, if necessary.

Purchase white table linens for buffet table, if desired.

Purchase dried wheat stalks for centerpiece, if desired.

Purchase favor boxes for Jordan almonds and tags to write baby's name on.

Arrange with a charitable organization or religious official to give charity before or during naming ceremony, if desired.

Contact religious leader or family member you'd like to recite special prayers or blessings, if desired.

One week before the event:

Buy groceries.

Make centerpiece for buffet table by placing dried wheat stalks in a large vase.

One day before the event:

Make Chicken Stuffed with Rice and Meat.

Make Stuffed Grape Leaves.

Make Eggplant Puree.

Make Beef and Cilantro *Kofta.*

Make Cracked Wheat with Yogurt.

Make Ali's Mother's Bread Pudding.

Store all items in refrigerator.
Set table.

Day of the event:
Make Lamb and Lavash Soup.
Make Mint Tea.
Reheat all menu items.

CHAPTER 7
Yemeni Sabbath Luncheon
(Ghada lil Youm Sebt)

Yemen is the most arable country in the Arabian Peninsula. Coffee, wheat, and corn all grow on the peaks of the Arabian plateau and are nourished by the strong rains of the summer monsoon season. Yemen is world renowned for its coffee and spices; Yemenis began roasting coffee in the thirteenth century. The English word "mocha," which denotes coffee flavoring, takes its name from the Yemeni port of the same name.

Yemenis love to eat hot, spicy foods. They have their own special spice mixes and hot sauce recipes, which help distinguish their cuisine from that of the rest of the Arabian Peninsula. Yemenis also enjoy special bread recipes for holidays: Muslims enjoy a bread called *Bint al Sahn* on Fridays and high holy days, while Jews prepare Sabbath bread to be eaten on Fridays, Saturdays, and high holy days.

Yemen was once home to a thriving Jewish community that traced its ancestry back to the Prophet Noah. While many of the recipes of the Yemeni Jewish community were also enjoyed by Yemeni Muslims, Sabbath recipes remained religiously significant. Many Yemeni expatriates took their love of spicy foods with them when they immigrated to other parts of the world.

This menu incorporates the Yemeni spice culture with Judaic traditions. It is simple to prepare, and since Judaism prohibits work on the Sabbath, the menu items can be made on Friday before sundown and on Saturday. Small burlap sacks and coffee (see the "Where to Buy Guide" for Arabian and Yemeni Coffees) are the theme of this event. If you can find them, handwoven baskets make excellent table decorations.

Menu
Spice Mix:
Yemeni Spice Mix (*Hawayij*)

Appetizers:
    Yemeni Sweet Sabbath Bread (*Kubaneh*)
    Fresh Fruit and Dates (purchased)
Soup:
    Tamar's Yemenite Chicken Soup (*Hasaa bil Dajaj*)
Drink:
    Arabian Cardamom Coffee (*Qahwa Arabeya*)
Favor:
    Yemeni Coffee

Yemeni Spice Mix (*Hawayij*)

This recipe comes from the book *Sephardic Israeli Cuisine: A Mediterranean Mosaic* written by my friend, Sheilah Kaufman, who is a cookbook author, food editor, cooking instructor, and lecturer. This spice mix is used in many Yemeni recipes. As with all spice mixes in the Arabian Peninsula, this mix varies based on price and availability of ingredients and personal preferences. I have seen other recipes using only cumin, turmeric, and black pepper. This version is more complex and balanced.

Ingredients:

6 teaspoons black peppercorns
3 teaspoons caraway seeds
1/2 teaspoon saffron threads
1/2 teaspoon cumin
1 teaspoon cardamom seeds[*]
2 teaspoons turmeric

Preparation:

Combine all ingredients except turmeric in a coffee or spice
    grinder. Mix together until combined. Stir in the tur-
    meric and store in a covered jar.
Makes 5 tablespoons.

---

[*] Cardamom seeds can be found inside whole cardamom pods. To release the seeds, crush the outer shell of the cardamom pod, remove the tiny black seeds, and discard the pod. If you cannot find cardamom pods, substitute ground cardamom, and stir in at the end with the turmeric.

Yemeni Sweet Sabbath Bread (*Kubaneh*)

This recipe is also from Sheilah Kaufman's *Sephardic Israeli Cuisine: A Mediterranean Mosaic.* Sheilah suggests serving the bread hot for breakfast by pulling off pieces and eating it with eggs and tomatoes.

Ingredients:

1 tablespoon active dry yeast
1 1/2 cups lukewarm water
3 tablespoons thick jam (apricot, orange, or your favorite)
4 to 5 cups all-purpose flour
1 tablespoon salt
3 tablespoons butter or margarine, melted
Hard cooked eggs (1 per person) (optional)
2 or 3 large tomatoes, sliced (optional)

Preparation:

Dissolve the yeast in lukewarm water and stir in the jam. Let the mixture sit for 5 minutes.

Place 4 cups of flour and salt in a mixing bowl and make a well in the center. Pour the yeast mixture into the well.

Using the dough hook on a standing mixer, or a wooden spoon, mix the dough until it is kneaded. Place it in a lightly oiled bowl, cover with a clean kitchen towel, and let rise for 1 hour.

Punch dough down, remove it from the bowl, place it on a work surface, and knead in as much of the remaining cup of flour as needed to make a smooth but slightly sticky dough. Return the dough to the bowl, cover, and let rise for another hour.

Rub some of the butter or margarine around the inside of a heavy 5- to 6-quart pot.

Punch down the dough and divide into 4 balls. Roll the balls around in the remaining melted butter or margarine and place in the bottom of the pot. Cover with a lid and let rise for another 30 minutes.

Preheat oven to 375°F. Place rack in the lowest position in the oven. Bake the bread, covered, in the pot for 30 minutes. Reduce heat to 150°F (or oven's lowest temperature) and continue baking overnight or for at least 8 hours.

Serves 12.

Tamar's Yemenite Chicken Soup (*Hasaa bil Dajaj*)

This soup is a true one-pot meal, chock full of chicken, vegetables, spices, and broth. It can be made ahead of time because it freezes well. It can also be found in Sheilah Kaufman's *Sephardic Israeli Cuisine: A Mediterranean Mosaic.*

Ingredients:

1 (4-pound) whole chicken, cut up
2 onions, peeled
4 to 6 carrots, peeled
1 bunch leeks, white bulbs and green tops divided
3 tablespoons fresh parsley, chopped
2 potatoes, peeled and cut into chunks
1 butternut squash, peeled and cut into 2x1-inch chunks
2 chicken bouillon cubes
2 to 2 1/2 teaspoons *Hawayij* (see page 98)
1 bunch fresh cilantro, washed with stems removed
Salt, to taste

Preparation:

Place chicken in a large pot and add enough cold water to cover plus an inch more. Bring to a boil over high heat. Reduce heat to medium, and as chicken cooks, skim off the scum, cook about 15 minutes. Add onion, carrots, white bulbs of the leeks, and parsley, cover and cook for 20 minutes. Add potatoes and squash and stir in bouillon cubes and spices. Lower heat to simmer, cover, and cook until chicken is done, about 45 minutes. Add cilantro and chopped greens from the leeks, stir, and cook another 10 minutes. Remove chicken from the pot, let soup cool, and strain the broth.

Keep chicken separate. Tear or cut into pieces and add to soup before serving, if desired, or freeze chicken for future use. If needed, add salt.

Serves 8.

Arabian Cardamom Coffee (*Qahwa Arabeya*)

As soon as lunch and dinner are over in the Arabian Peninsula, the cool, watery, scent of cardamom begins seeping out of
kitchens, filling the air with a sensuous spice blanket. Coffee is
an important part of daily life throughout the region. It symbol-
izes hospitality and is used to punctuate the beginning and end
of a meal.

Ground Arabic coffee is golden in color. It is mixed with equal
parts (or sometimes
even more) ground
cardamom. It tastes
like an herbal tea yet
offers the stimulant
properties of espresso.
Many people who do
not drink coffee but
who enjoy spices and
herbal teas find this
drink appealing.

I was hooked af-
ter one cup, so I imme-
diately went to a spice
shop in Mecca to buy
both the coffee and the
cardamom. Then, I
searched every *souq* I
came across until I
found my favorite
coffee pot. When my
husband's Saudi friend
Emad found out about
my love of Arabic cof-
fee, he brought me two
kilos of coffee and cardamom premixed, "so that I wouldn't have
to bother with it at home."

Arabic coffee is made in beautiful gold-, silver-, and copper-
colored pots with handles and spouts resembling Aladdin's lamp.
The pots are often decorated with jewels or designs. The coffee is
cooked over stoves or the coals of an open fire. It is served in

small eggshell-size porcelain cups without handles that resemble Japanese saki cups.

Ingredients:
3 cups water
3 tablespoons ground cardamom
2 tablespoons ground Arabic coffee*
Pinch of saffron, if desired

Preparation:
Combine water, cardamom, coffee, and saffron in a medium saucepan or Arabic coffee pot. Bring to a boil over medium-high heat. Reduce heat to low and simmer for 5 minutes. Strain into Arabic coffee cups. Serve hot with dates.
Serves 10.

Tip: Arabic coffee is never served with sugar. It is always served with dates, to balance the bitterness.

Entertaining Timeline

Two weeks before the event:
Invite friends and familiy.
Purchase Arabic coffee pot.
Mail order hard to find ingredients if necessary.
Purchase Arabic Cardamom Coffee and Yemeni Coffee.
Purchase small burlap sacks and twine or drawstring cheesecloth sachets from craft store.
Purchase plastic sandwich bags.
Place 1/2 cup Yemeni Coffee inside plastic sandwich bags, place bags in small burlap sacks or cheesecloth sachets, and fasten shut.

---

* See "Where to Buy Guide" for purchasing information for Arabic coffee and Arabic coffee cups.

Purchase handwoven baskets for Sweet Sabbath Bread and Fresh Fruit and Dates if necessary.

One week before the event:
Confirm number of guests and make grocery list accordingly.
Buy nonperishable items on grocery list.
Make Yemeni Sweet Sabbath Bread and freeze.
Make Yemeni Spice Mix and store in a glass jar.

Two days before the event:
Buy remaining groceries.
Make Tamar's Yemenite Chicken Soup and store in the refrigerator.

One day before the event:
Hard boil eggs and store in refrigerator.
Set table.
Arrange fresh fruit with dates in handwoven basket and use as centerpiece.
Place a coffee favor on top of each place setting.

Day of the event:
Remove Sweet Sabbath Bread from freezer to thaw.
Remove hard-boiled eggs and hot sauce from refrigerator and bring to room temperature.
Reheat soup and warm bread as guests arrive.
Make Arabic Cardamom Coffee and serve when guests arrive and again after lunch.

CHAPTER 8
Ramadan Breakfast (*Sohoor*)

Sohoor is the predawn breakfast eaten during the month of Ramadan. During the ninth month of the lunar Islamic calendar, adult Muslims who are physically able abstain from food and drink from sunup to sundown, a tradition begun by the Prophet Muhammad. Fasting during Ramadan is the fourth of the five pillars of Islam. During the month of Ramadan the *Torah*, *Bible*, and *Qur'an* were revealed. Fasting during daytime hours is supposed to increase Muslims' self-discipline and piety and encourage them to be more generous when giving charity (the third pillar of Islam) throughout the year.

Ceiling of the Great Mosque in Medina, Saudi Arabia.

To give them strength to make it through each day of fasting, Muslims eat and drink before sun up. Even a few dates and milk provide nutrition and can give the fasting person energy to last the day. Many families adjust their schedules during Ramadan to adhere to this tradition.

In many neighborhoods, men walk through the streets in the predawn hours chanting, "Wake up believers. Prayer is better than sleep." Then you'll hear pots and pans clanking, and lights from homes start to illuminate the streets. Families talk as they enjoy their morning meals together. A few minutes before dawn, everyone stops eating. The dawn calls to prayer sound from the minarets of nearby mosques, and everyone prepares to pray. Afterward many people read the *Qur'an* and make additional supplications. During vacations or days off of work and school, many people go to sleep after the morning prayer and wake up in the afternoon. Others go to school and work and rush home before the sunset prayer to enjoy meals with their families.

Traditionally, the menu items for the Ramadan breakfast are quick to prepare because they have to be made so early in the morning. Otherwise, they are started the night before and reheated the next day. You don't have to wait until Ramadan to enjoy these breakfast favorites; they taste great anytime. Try serving them as a late breakfast or brunch to houseguests. This menu also works well as a light dinner.

Menu

Saudi Pureed Fava Beans (*Fuul Medammes*)
Pita Bread (purchased)
Fried Eggs with Pastrami (*Beid bil Basterma*)
Tomato, Cucumber, and Carrot Salad (*Salata bil Tomatum, Khiyar wa Jazaar*)
Bread Topped with *Zataar* Spice Mix (*Manaqish*)
Plain Yogurt (purchased)
Assorted Cheeses (purchased)
Coffee
Tea

Saudi Pureed Fava Beans (*Fuul Medammes*)

Fava beans are believed to be the world's oldest agricultural crop. Saudi Arabia and many other Middle Eastern countries inherited this fava bean dish from Egypt. In Saudi Arabia, where it is prepared slightly differently than it is in Egypt, it is a popular breakfast dish. Recently, doctors in Egypt released research proving that a breakfast of Pureed Fava Beans, eggs, and pita bread provide all of the nutrients needed during a day's worth of activity. Needless to say, it is thus a popular choice for a predawn meal during Ramadan.

Ingredients:
1 tablespoon clarified butter (ghee)
1 (15-ounce) can cooked fava beans with juice
Juice of 1 lemon
1 teaspoon Saudi Spice Mix (See page 3)
Salt, to taste
1 hard-boiled egg, crumbled
2 roma tomatoes, diced

Preparation:
Heat clarified butter in a medium frying pan over medium-low heat. Add beans and juice from can, lemon juice, Saudi Spice Mix, and salt. Stir well to combine. Cook for 5 minutes or until most of the liquid is absorbed. Reduce heat to low and mash slightly with a fork or potato masher.
Spoon onto a serving plate. Top with crumbled egg and tomatoes. Serve with pita bread.
Serves 4 to 6.

Tip: This dish can also be eaten as a vegetarian lunch or dinner.

Fried Eggs with Pastrami (Beid bil Basterma)
Pastrami is a popular breakfast item in the Middle East.

Ingredients:
1 teaspoon corn oil
4 large eggs
4 pastrami slices
Salt, to taste
Freshly ground pepper, to taste

Preparation:
Heat oil in a large frying pan over low heat.

Crack eggs and arrange in pan. Cook over low heat until yolks begin to set. Top each egg with a slice of pastrami. Finish cooking eggs. Season with salt and pepper, if desired.

Serves 4.

Tomato, Cucumber, and Carrot Salad (*Salata bil Tomatum, Khiyar wa Jazaar*)

Breakfast salads in the Arabian Peninsula often consist of sliced fresh vegetables arranged in attractive patterns without dressing.

Ingredients:
2 ripe tomatoes
2 small cucumbers
2 carrots

Preparation:
Slice tomatoes into quarters. Arrange on 1/3 of a serving platter or large plate. Slice cucumbers in half lengthwise and widthwise. Arrange on another 1/3 of the plate. Peel carrots and quarter them. Arrange on remaining 1/3 of plate.

Serves 4.

Bread Topped with *Zataar* Spice Mix (*Manaqish*)

Manaqish is a Palestinian breakfast specialty that is likely to have come to the Arabian Peninsula with Palestinians who were making the pilgrimage to Mecca. Originally, women baked dough in communal ovens in the morning and prepared smaller portions of dough, which they topped with spices and eggs, so that they wouldn't have to make a separate breakfast.

Ingredients:
2 1/4 teaspoons active, dry, rapid-rise yeast
1 teaspoon salt
3 cups unbleached, all-purpose flour, plus extra for dusting work surface

1/4 cup extra-virgin olive oil, divided
1/3 cup *Zataar* Spice Mix (See page 64)

Preparation:

Stir yeast into 1/8 cup warm water. Allow to rest for 15 minutes.

In a large bowl, or in the bowl of a standing mixer, combine salt and flour. Add yeast mixture and mix to combine. While stirring, or while mixer is running, slowly add 1 cup of water to flour mixture. Mix well to incorporate all ingredients. Keep in mind that you may use more or less water depending on the humidity of the room you are baking the bread in.

Pour mixture out onto a lightly floured work surface. Shape the dough into a ball and knead it for 8 to 10 minutes, until dough is smooth and elastic.

Use 1 tablespoon of the olive oil to oil a large bowl. Place dough in the bowl and turn to coat. Cover with plastic wrap and kitchen towels. Set in a warm, draft-free area to rise until dough is doubled in size (1 1/2 to 2 hours).

When dough has risen, punch it down and turn it out onto a lightly floured work surface. (At this point, the dough can be wrapped in plastic wrap and refrigerated or frozen for a later use.) Sprinkle flour on top of dough and pinch off 15 (1-inch) pieces of dough. Form each piece into a ball.

Sprinkle a rolling pin with flour and roll each ball into a 3-inch round. Place on a lined or greased baking sheet. Brush tops of dough with olive oil and sprinkle generously with *Zataar* Spice Mix. Repeat until all dough is used. Cover with clean kitchen towels and allow to rest for 1 hour.

After 30 minutes have passed, preheat oven to 425°F.

Bake for 15 minutes, or until puffed and browned. Cool slightly and serve warm.

Serves 8 to 10.

Tip: You can serve Manaqish *topped with a good quality* labna *(yogurt cheese) in place of pizza.*

Entertaining Timeline

One week to one day before breakfast:
Invite guests.
Confirm number of guests and make grocery list accordingly.
Purchase groceries and specialty items.
Make and freeze Bread Topped with *Zataar* Spice Mix.

One night before the breakfast:
Remove Bread Topped with *Zataar* Spice Mix from freezer.
Make Tomato, Cucumber, and Carrot Salad.
Place yogurt and cheeses on serving platters and store in
    the refrigerator.
Set the table.

Morning of the breakfast:
Make Saudi Pureed Fava Beans.
Make Fried Eggs with Pastrami.
Make coffee and tea.

CHAPTER 9
Ramadan Dinner (*Iftaar*)

Iftaar is the meal eaten after sunset during Ramadan. This meal is greatly anticipated by Muslims who have fasted from sunup to sundown. Ramadan *iftaar* menus are a medley of the most beloved recipes of each Muslim culture. Many menu items are only prepared during Ramadan.

In Muslim countries, the end of a day's worth of fasting is marked with the sounding of a cannon. Mosque minarets begin calling the sundown prayer and everyone breaks their fast by drinking water and eating a few dates, a tradition started by the Prophet Muhammad. According to prophetic sayings, dates have more nutritional properties than any other fruit. Because they

The Great Mosque of Medina during Friday prayers.

are plentiful in the Arabian Peninsula, many delicious varieties are easy to come by. After breaking their fasts, Muslims say the sundown prayer and then sit down with their families to enjoy the much-anticipated *iftaar*.

Each culture and family prepares different dishes during Ramadan. The most important thing to remember when preparing *iftaar* is the meal should be complete and satisfying. It should meet not only the nutritional requirements of the fasting person but also his or her specific cravings. Special sweet treats are anticipated during Ramadan. After the meal, many families visit with relatives and perform extra prayers in the evening when streets are adorned with lanterns and decorative lights. Some stay awake until the dawn prayers. School and business schedules are often altered to enable people to enjoy Ramadan more easily.

This menu does not have a particular color theme. Any color could work. Many families do, however, use special glasses painted with Qur'anic inscriptions during Ramadan. A crescent moon with a star, the symbol of Islam, as well as images of Qur'ans and mosques are often seen in Ramadan decorations. The favor for this menu is dried dates. Giving dates as a gift is common during Ramadan. Prophet Muhammad said that anyone who gave so much as a date to a fasting person would be rewarded with heaven in the afterlife.

Keep in mind that Ramadan *iftaars* are usually informal affairs. This menu is ideal for entertaining during Ramadan because it includes so many options. For a regular family dinner, however, it could be simplified to one or two dishes per course.

Menu
Appetizers:
Macerated Dates (*Khoshaf*)
Saudi Beef *Sambusak* (*Sambusak bi Lahma*)
Pan-Fried Zucchini with Tahini Dressing (*Koosa bil Tahina*)

Soup:
Arabian Lamb, Vegetable, and Orzo Soup (*Hasaa Khodar*)

Main Courses:
Lamb with Hulled Grains (*Lahma Dani bil Freekeh*)

Chicken *Kabsah* (*Kabsah Dajaj*)
Lentils and Rice (*M'jadarah*)
Beef Stew with White Beans (*Tajin Lahma bi Fuul Abyud*)

Drink:
Apricot Juice (*Assir Q'amr Din*)

Desserts:
Sweet Nut-Filled Pancakes (*Qatayef*)
Delicate Fried Dough Windows with Syrup (*Mushabbak*)

Macerated Dates (*Khoshaf*)

Macerated dates are enjoyed in many Muslim countries during Ramadan because the Prophet Muhammad traditionally broke his fast with dates. Eating dates has thus become a symbolic Ramadan tradition. The word "dates" appears 248 times in the 146 *hadith* (the recorded sayings and actions of the Prophet Muhammad), according to the Bukhari translation. In seventh-century Arabia dates were used to settle debts, as offers of charity, and in entertaining. While *khoshaf* originally contained only water and dates, modern cooks combine various kinds of dried fruits, sugar, nuts, and coconut in their version of this drink.

Ingredients:
1 pound firm dried dates, pitted
1/2 pound raisins
1/2 pound dried apricots, chopped into small pieces
1/4 cup sugar
1 teaspoon orange blossom water
1 teaspoon rose water

Preparation:
Place dates, raisins, and apricots in a large bowl. Pour 4 cups of boiling water over them. Stir in sugar, orange blossom water, and rose water. Let stand until water reaches room temperature and fruit becomes tender. Serve in small ramekins or mugs with a spoon.
Serves 4.

Saudi Beef Sambusak (*Sambusak bil Lahma*)

Beef *sambusak* are standard fare in Saudi Arabia. I sampled them everywhere, from the guest palace in Mina to private residences in Mecca. The *sambusak* that I enjoyed the most, however, were served to me by my friend Batoul in her home just outside of Mecca. She prepared a traditional Saudi meal for us and invited her sisters to lunch to join us. Saudi custom dictates that nonrelated members of the opposite sex do not socialize together. So our husbands ate in one room while Batoul, her sisters, and I ate in another. Tablecloths were set out on the floor in a "dining room" that contained no furniture, and the beautiful freshly made meal was laid out in front of us. Dining on the floor is an honor in Saudi culture, one that is extended to guests.

Without the presence of men or chairs, we were able to have intimate discussions and came to know each other quite well. The lunch made such an impression on me that a few days later I told my husband, "We really have to have Batoul and her husband over for dinner this weekend." He looked at me in amazement and said, "They live in Mecca." We had just returned to America and apparently jet lag had gotten the better of me!

Ingredients:

3 cups unbleached, all-purpose flour, plus extra for dusting
1 teaspoon fennel seeds
1 teaspoon black poppy seeds
1 tablespoon active dry yeast
Salt, to taste
4 1/2 cups corn oil, divided
1 pound ground beef or lamb, rinsed and drained well
1 onion, peeled and diced
1 tablespoon Saudi Spice Mix (see page 3)

Preparation:

Place the flour in a large bowl. Add the fennel, poppy seeds, 1 teaspoon salt, and yeast. Add 1/2 cup corn oil and 1/2 cup lukewarm water and stir to combine well. Continue mixing until a dough forms. If mixture seems too sticky, add more flour, a tablespoon at a time. If mixture seems too dry, add more water, a tablespoon at a time.

Once dough is formed, divide into 8 equal pieces. Set onto a
lightly floured work surface in a warm, draft-free location. Cover with kitchen cloths and allow to rise for 1
hour.

Heat a large frying pan over medium heat. Add ground beef
or lamb, onion, and Saudi Spice Mix. Cook, stirring occasionally, until meat is browned. Remove from heat
and cool.

Once dough has risen, remove kitchen cloths. Lightly dust a
work surface and rolling pin. Roll the dough pieces out
into 4- to 5-inch circles.

Place 2 tablespoons of meat in the center of each round.
Fold in half to cover the meat and, using a fork, press
down around edges to seal.

Heat remaining 4 cups of corn oil in a large skillet. Fry the
sambusak for 3 to 5 minutes per side, or until golden.
Remove from oil with a slotted spoon and transfer to a
platter lined with paper towels. Serve hot.

Serves 6 to 8.

**Tip: If you don't have time to make fresh dough, you can
substitute wonton wrappers or phyllo dough.**

Pan-Fried Zucchini with Tahini Dressing (*Koosa bil
Tahina*)

Dressing pan-fried vegetables with tahini is both sumptuous and healthy. Eggplant, peppers, and cauliflower can be sliced
and substituted or served in addition to the zucchini in this recipe.
Try serving this dish as an accompaniment to grilled or roasted
meats.

Ingredients:
3 small zucchini
1/8 cup canola oil
1/4 cup tahini (sesame paste)
Juice of 1 lemon
1 teaspoon olive oil
Salt, to taste
Freshly ground pepper, to taste

Preparation:

Slice zucchini in half lengthwise. Slice in half lengthwise again. Slice each stick in half widthwise to make thin sticks.

Heat canola oil over medium-high heat in a large, shallow frying pan. When oil is hot, add zucchini sticks. Fry for 3 to 5 minutes on each side, until golden brown and tender. Remove from oil and place on a platter lined with paper towels.

In a blender, or a mixing bowl, whisk together tahini, lemon juice, olive oil, and salt and pepper to form a dressing. If dressing is too thick, add water, a tablespoon at a time, to smooth it out. Taste dressing and adjust seasonings, if necessary.

Pour most of dressing out onto the bottom of a serving dish. Spread around to coat the entire bottom. Arrange zucchini on top of serving platter. Spoon remaining dressing on top of zucchini. Serve warm or at room temperature.

Serves 4.

Tip: Look for firm, bright green zucchini without bruises for the best results.

Arabian Lamb, Vegetable, and Orzo Soup (Hasaa Khodar)

The original version of this classic meal in a pot contained incense. It is common in the Arabian Peninsula to add a small piece of incense or fragrance to slow-cooking soups. Pure resins like frankincense are safe to eat and were once used as chewing gum is today. During cooking, the incense fragrance rises into the air and mingles with the spice in the food for a delightful effect. This version uses dried lemon and saffron instead of incense.

Ingredients:

3 cloves
3 green cardamom pods
1 dried lemon*

---

* See "Where to Buy Guide" for purchasing information.

3 strands saffron
1 pound boneless lamb shoulder, cubed
Salt, to taste
Freshly ground pepper, to taste
3 zucchinis, cut into 1-inch pieces
3 carrots, cut into 1-inch pieces
3 potatoes, cut into 1-inch pieces
1 tablespoon tomato paste
1 cup orzo pasta

Preparation:
Wrap cloves and cardamom pods in a cheesecloth sack and
  secure with butcher's twine.
Bring 12 cups of water to a boil over high heat in a large
  stockpot. Add cheesecloth sack, dried lemon, saffron,
  lamb, salt, and freshly ground pepper. Allow mixture
  to boil for 1 minute, reduce heat to very low, and simmer, covered, for 1 hour.
Add zucchini, carrot, potato, and tomato paste. Stir well and
  continue to simmer, covered, for 30 minutes.
Stir in orzo and simmer, uncovered, until orzo is al dente
  (10 to 15) minutes.
Taste and adjust seasonings, if necessary. Remove cheesecloth and dried lemon and discard. Serve warm.
Serves 6 to 8.

Tip: This soup can be made in large batches and frozen.

Lamb with Hulled Grains
(Lahma Dani bil Freekeh)
Hulled grain is a common ingredient in Middle Eastern
dishes. It has a smoky taste that adds to the richness of lamb
dishes. Hulled grain is traditionally accompanied by plain
yogurt.

Ingredients:
6 tablespoons clarified butter (ghee), divided
6 lamb shanks, ends trimmed down
6 cups chicken stock

2 tablespoons Saudi Spice Mix (see page 3)
3 green cardamom pods, cracked
1 teaspoon salt
1 onion, diced
3 cups hulled grain, rinsed*
1/8 cup shelled pistachios
1/8 cup blanched almonds
1/8 cup pine nuts
1/4 cup raisins
1 cup plain yogurt, to serve

Preparation:

Melt 3 tablespoons clarified butter in a large, deep frying
pan over medium heat. Add lamb shanks and brown on
all sides. Add stock, Saudi Spice Mix, cardamom pods,
and 1 teaspoon salt. Mix well. Increase heat to high
and bring mixture to a boil. Stir. Reduce heat to low,
cover, and simmer for 1 1/2 to 2 hours, or until meat is
tender. Remove meat from the frying pan, cover to keep
warm, and strain broth into a large bowl.

Melt remaining 3 tablespoons of clarified butter in the same
frying pan over medium heat. Add onion and sauté until
translucent (3 to 5 minutes). Add hulled grain to the
pan and stir to incorporate with onions. Add 5 1/2 cups
of reserved broth to the pan. If less than 5 1/2 cups of
broth remain from cooking the lamb, use water to make
up the difference.

Increase heat to high and bring to a boil. Reduce heat to
low, cover and cook for approximately 40 minutes to 1
hour, until all liquid is absorbed and grain is tender.

Before grains finish cooking, place a small frying pan over
medium heat. Add pistachios, almonds, pine nuts, and
raisins. Fry, stirring constantly, until nuts turn golden
and begin to release an aroma. Take off heat.

Pour grains out onto a serving dish and arrange lamb shanks
on top. Sprinkle with fried nuts and raisins. Serve

---

*   See "Where to Buy Guide" for purchasing information.

warm with plain yogurt on the side.
Serves 4 to 6.

Tip: When you have time, fry large batches of nuts and raisins in advance, and store them in the refrigerator so they will be ready for dishes like this when you need them.

Chicken Kabsah (*Kabsah Dajaj*)

This famous Saudi dish tastes as great the next day as it does the day it's cooked. Be sure to use an attractive frying pan and serve *kabsah* directly from it at the table.

Ingredients:
1 tablespoon clarified butter (ghee)
1 small chicken, cut up or 2 1/2 pounds chicken thighs
1 onion, diced
4 garlic cloves, diced
3/4 cup tomato puree
1 tablespoon Saudi Spice Mix (see page 3)
Salt, to taste
3 cups chicken stock
1 cup basmati rice, soaked for 15 minutes and rinsed
1 tablespoon corn oil
1/4 cup raisins
1/4 cup blanched almonds, slivered

Preparation:
Melt clarified butter in a large, nonstick frying pan over medium heat. Add chicken pieces and brown on all sides. Add onion and sauté until translucent. Add garlic and stir. Add tomato puree, Saudi Spice Mix, and salt. Cook together for 1 minute and add stock. Increase heat to high and bring to a boil. Reduce heat to low and cover. Simmer for 45 minutes. Stir rice in between chicken pieces and cover. Continue to simmer for 20 to 30 minutes, or until rice is tender and liquid is absorbed.
Heat corn oil in a small frying pan over low heat. Fry raisins and almonds until almonds turn light golden and

begin to release their aroma. Spoon raisins and nuts over chicken and rice and serve hot.

Serves 4 to 6.

Tip: Packaged or canned chicken stock can be substituted for fresh stock in this recipe.

Lentils and Rice (M'jadarah)

M'jadarah is a dish found in most Arab countries. It is a simple, delicious vegetarian main course. If you do not like cumin, you can flavor the rice with dried coriander instead.

Ingredients:
3/4 cup lentils, rinsed and sorted
3 cups chicken or vegetable stock, or water
Salt, to taste
Freshly ground pepper, to taste
1 1/2 cups basmati rice
1 teaspoon cumin
1/4 cup olive or corn oil
2 large onions, quartered and sliced
1 lemon, sliced into 4 wedges

Preparation:
In a medium saucepan, combine lentils, stock or water, and salt and pepper. Cook uncovered for 15 minutes on medium heat. Add rice and cumin and mix well. Reduce heat to low and cover. Cook until rice is tender and liquid is absorbed, 20 to 30 minutes.

While rice is cooking, heat olive or corn oil over medium heat in a large frying pan. Add onion slices in a single layer and sauté until dark golden and tender, about 10 minutes. Set aside.

When rice is finished cooking, fluff with a fork and turn out onto a serving platter. Taste and add salt, if necessary. Pour oil and onions on top to garnish. Serve hot, with lemon wedges.

Serves 4.

Tip: This can be accompanied by Cilantro Salad (see page 150) and Cucumber and Yogurt Salad (see page 33) as a meal on a busy weeknight.

Beef Stew with White Beans
(Tajin Lahma bi Fuul Abyud)

This is one of the many fantastic dishes I was served at the Jeddah Conference Palace in Saudi Arabia. This dish is traditionally served with *Khaleeji* White Rice (see page 160) and/or Cracked Wheat (see page 90) and salad. Keep in mind that the dried beans used in this dish need to be soaked overnight.

Ingredients:

2 tablespoons clarified butter (ghee) or corn oil
1 medium onion, finely chopped
2 pounds boneless beef shoulder, cubed
Salt, to taste
1 tablespoon Saudi Spice Mix (See page 3)
1 teaspoon sugar
2 cups chicken or beef stock
1 (1-pound) bag dry white beans, soaked overnight, rinsed, and drained

Preparation:

Heat clarified butter or oil in a large saucepan over medium heat. Add onions and sauté until translucent, 3 to 5 minutes. Add beef and brown on all sides. Stir in salt, Saudi Spice Mix, and sugar. Add 2 cups water and stock, stir, and add white beans. Increase heat to high and bring to a boil. Reduce heat to medium low, cover, and simmer 1 1/2 to 2 hours, or until meat and beans are tender. Serve warm.

Serves 4 to 6.

Tip: You may substitute canned white beans, which have been rinsed well and drained, for the dried beans in this recipe. Veal or lamb meat could be used instead of beef, if desired.

Apricot Juice (Assir Q'amr Din)

Apricots were originally grown in China. They arrived in the Arabian Peninsula with the Persians and quickly became extremely popular. At one time, Damascus, Syria, produced more than twenty-one different kinds of apricots. Twelve of them became extinct, and currently only nine varieties are produced. They are still considered to be of superior quality by people in the Arab world.

The Arabic term for dried apricot, *q'amr din*, literally translates as "moon of faith." In Arabian countries, dried fruits were traditionally reserved for Ramadan. After a long day's fast, nothing is more refreshing than sweet apricot juice, and making it from scratch is very easy. This is a fun project for kids. When I was a child, I remember being particularly fond of one of my aunts who always offered me apricot juice when I went to her home.

Ingredients:
1 pound dried apricots, chopped into small pieces
1 cup sugar

Preparation:
Place chopped apricots in a large, heat-proof bowl and cover
   them with 6 cups boiling water. When the apricot pieces
   dissolve, stir in sugar until it also dissolves. Puree the
   mixture in a blender. Refrigerate until cold.
Serves 6.

Sweet Nut-Filled Pancakes (Qatayef)

In many parts of the Middle East, *qatayef* are synonymous with Ramadan. As Muslims begin their fast at sunup each morning, the *qatayef* makers are already busy at work. Walking down an average street, you'll see bakers pouring pancake batter onto griddles, stuffing the pancakes with mixed nuts or cream, and baking or deep-frying them. Ultimately, they're drenched in a sweet syrup. I prefer the tender texture of baked *qatayef* to the fried variety. If you choose to fry them, use the recipe that follows, but instead of putting the pancakes in the oven, fry them in 2 inches of corn oil until golden.

Ingredients:

For the batter:
1 1/2 teaspoons active dry yeast
1 1/2 teaspoons sugar
2 cups unbleached, all-purpose flour
1/8 teaspoon salt
Canola oil, for frying
For the syrup:
1 cup sugar
Juice of 1/2 lemon
3 strips lemon peel
1/2 teaspoon or-
    ange blos-
    som water
1/2 teaspoon rose
    water
For the filling:
1/4 cup blanched
    a l m o n d s ,
    ground
1/4 cup walnuts,
    ground

Sweet Nut-Filled Pancakes

Preparation:

Mix yeast with sugar and 1/4 cup warm water. Stir until
    yeast and sugar have dissolved.
Sift flour and salt into a large mixing bowl. Make a well in
    the center. Pour in yeast mixture and 1 1/4 cups warm
    water. Whisk until batter becomes smooth. Cover bowl
    with plastic wrap and kitchen towels and place in a
    warm, draft-free area. Let rise for 1 hour. Batter is ready
    when it is bubbly.
In the meantime, prepare the syrup: Combine 3/4 cup wa-
    ter with sugar, lemon juice, and zest in a medium
    saucepan. Stir and cook over medium-high heat, dis-
    solving sugar and stirring often. Bring mixture to a
    boil, stop stirring, and lower heat to medium low.
    Allow mixture to cook for 10 minutes. Take off of heat
    and set aside to cool. Remove lemon peel and discard.

Stir in orange blossom water and rose water.

When batter is ready, heat 1/4 inch of canola oil in a large frying pan.

Preheat oven to 350°F.

Carefully pour 1 heaping tablespoon of batter into the oil to form a 4-inch circle-shaped pancake. Continue with remaining batter, be careful not to crowd pan. When top of pancakes are full of holes, remove them with a spatula and place on a paper towel-lined tray, cooked side down.

When all of the batter has been used, begin to fill the pancakes. Mix ground almonds and walnuts together. Pour 1/2 teaspoon on the uncooked side of the pancake. Fold the pancake in half around the stuffing, and pinch the edges together to seal. Place pancakes together in a 10-inch oval-shaped baking pan. Continue filling and sealing the remaining pancakes. Snuggle each one into the pan with the others, until all pancakes have been filled and the pan is full. Bake for 30 to 40 minutes, or until pancakes are golden.

Remove from the oven and pour syrup over the top. Cool enough to handle and serve warm.

Serves 8 to 10. Makes 24.

Tip: Make syrup, filling, and pancake batter a day ahead, store in the refrigerator, and assemble and bake the qatayef *on the day of serving.*

Delicate Fried Dough Windows with Syrup (Mushabbak)

Mushabbak means "windows" in Arabic. This dessert is made by pouring batter into pretzel-like shapes, frying them in hot oil, and then drenching them in sweet syrup. The holes in the pretzel shapes are considered the "windows."

Ingredients:
For the syrup:
2 cups sugar
1 teaspoon lemon juice
1 strip lemon peel

Red food coloring, if desired
For the batter:
1 cup unbleached, all-purpose flour
1/2 cup cornmeal
1 tablespoon active dry yeast
2 cups canola or corn oil, for frying

Preparation:

Prepare the syrup by combining the sugar, 1 cup water, lemon juice, and lemon peel in a medium saucepan. Bring to a boil, stirring, over medium heat. Once sugar dissolves, stop stirring. Reduce heat to low and simmer, uncovered, for 10 minutes. Remove from heat to cool. Remove lemon peel and discard. Pour 1/4 cup of syrup into a small bowl. Add a few drops of red food coloring and stir well. Set aside.

To make batter, combine flour, cornmeal, yeast, and 1 cup water in a large bowl. Mix well to form a dough. If dough seems too thick (it should be slightly thicker than pancake batter), add more water, a tablespoon at a time.

Pour oil into a large frying pan over medium heat. Heat oil to 365°F.

Spoon the dough into a pastry bag fitted with a smooth, round metal tip. With your finger on the end of the tip, using your hands on the side of the pastry bag, press the dough down to the bottom of the bag and twist the top of the bag to keep pressure on the dough. Carefully pipe dough into oil, squeezing it into pretzel-like shapes. Fry for about 2 minutes per side, or until golden.

With a large, slotted spoon, remove from hot oil onto dishes lined with paper towels. Pour syrup into a large bowl. Place *Mushabbak* in syrup and turn to coat. If desired, dip part of window in colored syrup, so that 1/2 of window is red and 1/2 is natural colored. Repeat until all dough is used. Serve hot or at room temperature.

Serves 4 to 6.

Tip: If you don't have a pastry bag to use for piping the batter, put the batter in a plastic sandwich bag and snip off the end.

Entertaining Timeline

One week to one day before the dinner:
Invite friends and family.
Confirm number of guests and make grocery list accordingly.
Buy groceries.

One day before the dinner:
Make Apricot Juice and Macerated Dates and store in
    refrigerator.
Make Arabian Lamb, Vegetable, and Orzo Soup and store in
    refrigerator.
Make Saudi Beef *Sambusak* and store in refrigerator.
Make Beef Stew with White Beans and store in refrigerator.
Make Pan-Fried Zucchini.
Set table.

Day of the dinner:
Make Sweet Nut-Filled Pancakes.
Make Delicate Fried Dough Windows with Syrup.
Make Lamb with Hulled Grains.
Make Lentils and Rice.
Make Chicken *Kabsah*.

PART 3
SIMPLER DELIGHTS

Omani Incense Party (*Istakbal*)

Arabian "Mocktail" Party

Children's Pearl Diving Party

Bedouin Desert Truffle Party

Jeddah Red Sea Picnic

Oasis Date Harvest

Arabian Dessert Party

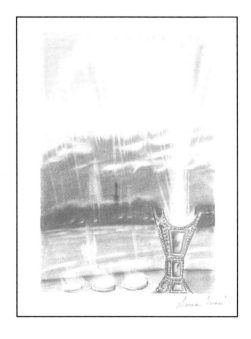

CHAPTER 10

Omani Incense Party (Istakbal)

The Omani incense party is designed to follow the format of an *istakbal*. *Istakbals* are gatherings meant to help friends keep abreast of what's happening in one another's lives. In the Middle East, they are common. Groups of female friends and neighbors often get together at one another's homes at a set time, usually once a month. During these meetings they catch up with one another, offer support, and of course, enjoy great food.

Istakbal menus range from simple assortments of tea or coffee and dates to large buffets. I have known Arabic women who immigrated to the United States who still hold *Istakbals* faithfully every month in order to stay in touch with friends from back home, who have also immigrated, while introducing their culture to new American friends.

I strongly believe that *istakbals* are an important social in-stitution for women as they provide nourishment, support, and companionship. Making a point to carry on the *istakbal* tradi-tion despite hectic schedules pays off in moral support. By rotat-ing hostesses, you'll learn many great recipes too.

Some hosts choose themes for their *istakbals*. In this book, the theme is the incense from the beautiful country of Oman. This theme will allow you to introduce your friends to a new cuisine and culture.

Incense permeates life in the Arabian Peninsula, where scented smoke is always wafting through the air. According to Kathleen Ammalee Rogers, a mind-body practitioner, renowned author, and speaker who has dedicated her life to helping others live their dreams, incense appeals to the right side of our brains; it opens up channels of communication for love, faith, and cre-ativity. I have seen incense used to perfume elevators, cleanse the streets outside of cafés, and scent the steam coming from a bathroom shower. Arabians use incense to set atmosphere the way Americans use lighting and/or music.

In Oman, at the end of a meal, an incense censor is passed around on a tray along with samples of pure fragrances. Guests wave the scented smoke onto themselves and then dab themselves with perfume before going outdoors. This signals that the dinner has come to an end, and it is time to leave.

Creating your own incense and fragrance tray is fun. First, you will need to choose a censor and an incense fragrance. Many people prefer incense sticks but be aware that they

Spice market featuring herbs, spices, incense, and laundry detergents.

contain chemicals that may cause respiratory health problems. Instead of sticks, opt for noncombustible incense, which can be found at health food and incense supply stores (see the "Where to Buy Guide" for details).

Frankincense and myrrh are traditional Omani scents. They burn for a long time and will create a balanced atmosphere for your party.

Preparation for this party is easy. Purchase your incense burner and supplies and make the Omani Spice Mix in advance. Once you have all of your ingredients, the rest of the meal can be made in a few hours' time.

Menu

Spice Mix:
>   Omani Spice Mix (*Bizaar*)

Salad:
>   Parsley Salad (*Salata Baqdounis*)

Main Courses:
>   Fish in Coconut Sauce (*Samak bil Salsa Narjeel*)
>   Meat and Rice (*Kabouli*)

Drink:
Omani Coffee (*Qahwa*)
Dessert:
Sweet Mouthfuls with Spiced Syrup (*Loquemat*)
Favor:
Incense woods wrapped in tulle circles[*]

Omani Spice Mix (*Bizaar*)

Bizaar is essential when cooking Omani cuisine and is great for spicing up ordinary dishes such as roasted chicken and lamb chops. In ancient times, the spices in this mix were roasted and blended to smooth consistencies. This recipe calls for pre-ground spices, making the mix easier to achieve in modern households. If desired, you can make the mix without the chili powder and coriander.

Ingredients:
1 tablespoon ground cardamom
4 tablespoons ground cinnamon
6 tablespoons ground coriander
2 tablespoons ground black pepper
1 teaspoon ground chili pepper
2 tablespoons ground cumin
1 teaspoon cloves

Preparation:
Mix all ingredients in a jar or blender until combined. Store in a jar with a tight-fitting lid.
Makes approximately 1 cup.

Tip: Let your taste buds be your guide: omit spices you don't like and add those you do.

Parsley Salad (*Salata Baqdounis*)

This healthful and versatile salad can be used for many occasions. To make this salad in advance, store both salad and

---

[*]   See "Where to Buy Guide" for purchasing information.

dressing, covered, separately in the refrigerator. Toss to combine before serving.

Ingredients:
1 bunch flat leaf parsley, finely chopped
4 roma tomatoes, diced
1 hot green pepper, diced
1 small cucumber, diced
1/4 cup extra-virgin olive oil
Juice of 1 lemon
Salt, to taste
Freshly ground pepper, to taste

Preparation:
Combine parsley, tomatoes, hot pepper, and cucumber in a medium bowl. Add olive oil, lemon juice, salt, and pepper. Toss well to combine. Serve at room temperature.
Serves 4.

Fish in Coconut Sauce (*Samak bil Salsa Narjeel*)

It is said that the fishermen and traders from Oman learned this recipe during their travels to the fabled spice island of Zanzibar, where coconut-infused seafood is an integral part of the cuisine. Omanis once ruled Zanzibar; by the nineteenth century, they had created a wealthy empire on the island, where ivory, gold, and spices were traded. The coastal areas of Oman contain many fishing villages and offer some of the most delicious fish in the world. The Arabian Sea is full of grouper, snapper, kingfish, tuna, shark, sardines, anchovies, and many other delicacies.

Traditionally the fish in this dish is cooked directly in the coconut sauce. In this version fish fillets are pan fried and served with the coconut sauce on the side. This recipe works particularly well with grouper, snapper, or tuna. Keep in mind that the fish needs to marinate for at least 2 hours or overnight.

Ingredients:

1 teaspoon ground ginger
1 teaspoon Omani Spice Mix (see page 130)
Salt, to taste
Juice and zest of 3 limes
2 pounds white fish fillets
4 garlic cloves, minced
3 cups coconut milk
1 cup plain dry breadcrumbs
2 tablespoons canola or corn oil
1/2 teaspoon ground cardamom

Preparation:

Combine ginger, Omani Spice Mix, salt, and lime juice and zest in a large shallow bowl. Add fish and turn to coat on all sides. Cover and refrigerate for 2 hours or overnight.

Meanwhile, make the coconut sauce by combining garlic, 2 cups of water, and coconut milk in a medium saucepan. Cook over low heat for 1 1/2 hours, stirring occasionally. Set aside. (This can be done a day ahead.)

After fish has marinated, remove from the refrigerator and place in a colander to drain off excess marinade.

Preheat oven to 400°F.

Pour breadcrumbs out onto a plate and dredge fish fillets in breadcrumbs to coat. Place on a plate.

Heat canola or corn oil in a large, ovenproof frying pan on medium heat. Add fish and brown on all sides. Place pan in oven and bake 20 to 25 minutes, or until fish is golden and cooked through.

Stir cardamom into coconut milk. Taste and season with salt.

Place fish on a serving platter with sauce on the side. Serve warm.

Serves 4 to 6.

Tip: Prepare the sauce and marinate the fish a night ahead of time. Store in the refrigerator until needed.

Meat and Rice (*Kabouli*)

Kabouli is the Omani version of Saudi *Kabsah*.

Ingredients:

1 tablespoon clarified butter (ghee)
1 onion, diced
1 1/2 pounds boneless lamb shoulder, cubed
1 clove garlic, minced
4 whole green cardamom pods, crushed
4 whole cloves
9 whole peppercorns
1 cinnamon stick
1 dried lime*
2 teaspoons Omani Spice Mix (see page 130)
Salt, to taste
1 1/4 cups basmati rice, soaked for 20 minutes and drained
1/2 cup raisins
1 lime, sliced, for garnish

Preparation:

Melt clarified butter in a large saucepan over medium heat. Add onion and sauté until translucent, 3 to 5 minutes. Add lamb shoulder and brown on all sides. Add garlic, cardamom pods, cloves, peppercorns, cinnamon stick, and dried lime and mix well. Cover meat with water, increase heat to high, and bring to a boil. Reduce heat to low and simmer, covered, for 1 1/2 hours.

Remove meat from pot and place on a plate. Strain broth into a bowl and discard spices and dried lime.

Return broth to the saucepan and stir in meat. Add the Omani Spice Mix and stir. (At this point, the dish could be refrigerated overnight and restarted the next day.) Add salt. Turn heat to high and bring mixture to a boil. Stir in rice, reduce heat to low, cover, and cook for 20 minutes or until water is absorbed.

While rice is cooking, heat a small frying pan and add

---

* See "Where to Buy Guide" for purchasing information.

raisins. Fry until warm and slightly puffed. Set aside. When meat and rice are finished, turn them out onto a serving platter. Garnish with raisins and lime slices. Serve hot. *Serves 4.*

Omani Coffee (Qahwa)

Coffee is a national institution in Oman. Always offered with dates and sometimes with other fresh fruits, Omani coffee contains fresh lightly roasted coffee beans, cardamom, and saffron. It is served in the same small eggshell-shaped cups used for Arabic Cardamom Coffee (see page 101). Guests usually wave the cups back and forth quickly to signal to their host that they've had enough. It is customary to drink up to three cups at one time. In Oman, coffee signals the beginning and end of a party.

Ingredients:
2 tablespoons ground cardamom
2 tablespoons ground Arabic coffee*
1/2 teaspoon saffron

Preparation:
Combine 2 cups water, cardamom, coffee, and saffron in a medium saucepan or Arabic coffee pot. Bring to a boil over medium-high heat. Reduce heat to low and simmer for 5 minutes. Strain and serve in Arabic coffee cups. *Serves 10.*

Sweet Mouthfuls with Spiced Syrup (Loquemat)

These Sweet Mouthfuls are fried until crisp and then soaked in a fragrant spice bath. The scent of the syrup alone makes this dessert worth the effort.

Ingredients:
For the syrup:
3/4 cup sugar

---

* See "Where to Buy Guide" for purchasing information for Arabic coffee and Arabic coffee cups.

1 teaspoon rose water
Juice of 1 lime
1/2 teaspoon ground cardamom
1/4 teaspoon saffron, crushed
For the Sweet Mouthfuls:
1 1/8 teaspoons active dry yeast mixed with a teaspoon of
    sugar
2 1/4 cups unbleached, all-purpose flour
1 tablespoon rice flour
1 large egg, beaten
1 tablespoon clarified butter (ghee)
4 cups corn oil, for frying

Preparation:

To make the syrup, combine 1 cup water and sugar in a
large saucepan. Stir and bring to a boil, uncovered, over
medium heat. Once syrup begins to boil, reduce heat to
low, discontinue stirring, and allow syrup to simmer
for 10 minutes. Stir in rose water, lime juice, cardamom, and saffron and set aside to cool.

To make the Sweet Mouthfuls, dissolve yeast and sugar
mixture in 1/4 cup lukewarm water in a small bowl.
Let rest 15 minutes, or until bubbly and doubled in
volume (this is called proofing the yeast).

In a large bowl, combine flour, rice flour, proofed yeast mixture, egg, and clarified butter with 1 3/4 cups water.
Mix to combine well, then whisk to remove lumps. Mixture should resemble a pancake batter. If batter seems
too thick, add more water, a tablespoon at a time, until
it is smooth. If batter seems too thin, add more flour, a
tablespoon at a time, until it is smooth. Cover with a
clean kitchen cloth, and then wrap entire bowl in a
clean towel. Set in a warm, draft-free place for 2
hours, or until batter is bubbly and has doubled in
volume.

When batter is ready, heat oil in a large saucepan. Use
two teaspoons to shape mouthfuls: grab the dough with
one teaspoon and push it off the teaspoon, onto work
surface, with the other.

When oil reaches 350 to 365°F, carefully drop the small balls into the hot oil (you may wear oven mitts while doing this). Fry 2 to 3 minutes per side, until golden brown. Remove with a slotted spoon onto a platter lined with paper towels.

Gently turn mouthfuls in syrup to coat and arrange on a serving platter.

Serve warm with Arabic coffee.

Serves 6 to 8.

Tip: *You can make the syrup up to 1 month in advance and store it in an airtight container in the refrigerator.*

Entertaining Timeline

One month to one week before party:
Invite guests.

Purchase incense censor, incense, and supplies.*

Purchase tulle circles from craft store to make favors.

Make Omani Spice Mix.

Make spiced syrup for Sweet Mouthfuls.

Purchase Arabic coffee, Arabic coffee pot, and Arabic coffee cups, if needed.

Purchase bottles of perfume oils, if needed.*

One week before the party:
Confirm number of guests and make grocery list accordingly.

Practice using incense burner, if needed.

Make favors by filling tulle circles with some incense and tying to seal.

Two days before the party:
Buy groceries.

---

* See "Where to Buy Guide" for purchasing information for incense censor, incense, Arabic coffee, Arabic coffee cups, and perfume oils.

One day before the party:

Make first part of Meat and Rice and refrigerate.

Marinate fish for Fish in Coconut Sauce.

Make coconut sauce for Fish in Coconut Sauce and refrigerate.

Make Parsley Salad and refrigerate salad and dressing separately.

Four hours before party:

Make Sweet Mouthfuls.

Finish making Fish in Coconut Sauce.

Toss Parsley Salad and dressing together.

Finish making Meat and Rice.

Before guests arrive:

Make Omani Coffee and serve to guests with dates as they arrive.

After the meal:

Make more Omani Coffee and serve to guests with Sweet Mouthfuls in Spiced Syrup and more dates.

Light incense censor, pass it around on tray with perfume oils to guests, and explain the Omani tradition.

CHAPTER 11
Arabian "Mocktail" Party

Sweet, delicious, and inventive fruit cocktails are served up all over the Arabian Peninsula. I have created the Arabian Mocktail Party around those family-friendly favorites. In addition to drinks, the menu is full of fantastic finger foods that taste great and are easy to prepare. These dishes could be passed around on trays or set out buffet-style for an open house.

Fruit vendor offerings (clockwise from top left): limes, golden apples, apricots, peaches, papayas, mangoes, pears, pink lady apples, artichokes, and pomegranates.

Although this menu will taste wonderful anytime, the combination of fruity and spicy flavors makes it most appropriate for a warm weather evening party. Use it for birthdays, open houses, showers, and housewarmings. This menu can be made almost entirely in advance, so all you need to do on the day of the party is mix the drinks, fry the shrimp, and serve your guests.

The décor for the party should be modern and artistic. Decorate with dishes with geometric patterns and table linens with bright, bold colors like red, white, orange, fuchsia, purple, and black. Create a centerpiece to match your linens using tropical flowers like birds of paradise, mimosas, and gladiolas. Play upbeat Arabic pop music, if desired.

Menu
Appetizers:
Red Lentil Dip (*Fattat Ads*)
Mini Chicken Pita Sandwiches (*Shwarma bil Dajaj*)
Mini Lamb Pita Sandwiches (*Shwarma bil Lahma Dani*)
Saudi Spiced Prawns (*Jamberi Saudi*)
Soup:
Roasted Red Pepper and Tomato Soup (*Hasaa Filfil
Ahmar wa Tomatum*)
Drinks:
Sunset Cocktail (*Cocktail Aghrub Ashams*)
Red Sky Cocktail (*Cocktail Asama'Hamra'a*)
Kiwi Cocktail (*Cocktail bil Kiwi*)
Dessert:
Almond Baklava (*Ba'lawa bil Lowz*)
Favor:
Spice jars filled with Saudi Spice Mix (see page 3)

Red Lentil Dip (*Fattat Ads*)
This is a quick and flavorful way to serve red lentils, which
do not need to cook as long as other lentil varieties do. In the
traditional dish, lentil puree is placed on top of fried pita pieces
and garnished with fried garlic. Instead, I like to serve the puree
as a dip with toasted pita wedges. The yogurt or sour cream garnish makes this dish even more delicious.

Ingredients:
1 cup dried red lentils, sorted and rinsed
2 cups vegetable or chicken stock
1 tablespoon tomato paste
5 garlic cloves, chopped
Salt, to taste
Freshly ground pepper, to taste
1 tablespoon ground coriander
4 loaves pita bread, quartered
1/4 cup plain yogurt or sour cream, for garnish
1 tablespoon cilantro, for garnish

Preparation:

Combine lentils, stock, tomato paste, garlic cloves, salt, and freshly ground pepper in a medium saucepan. Bring to a boil over high heat. Stir, reduce heat to low, and cover. Simmer for approximately 20 minutes, or until lentils are tender and all liquid is absorbed.

Transfer lentil mixture to food processor and pulse on and off to form a paste. Return lentil puree to saucepan and stir in coriander. Taste and adjust seasonings if necessary. Keep warm over low heat.

Toast pita wedges under broiler until golden, 1 to 2 minutes per side.

Place red lentil puree in a small bowl. Garnish with yogurt or sour cream and top with cilantro.

Arrange pita wedges on a plate and serve warm.

Serves 4.

Mini Chicken Pita Sandwiches (*Shwarma bil Dajaj*)

Shwarma is the rotisserie-cooked meat that is "shaved" and piled high in sandwiches all over the Middle East. Traditionally, the meat is threaded with layers of fat, topped with tomatoes and/or peppers, and left to cook slowly for hours. Needless to say it is tender, succulent, and full of flavor. This recipe enables you to enjoy this popular street food at home, saving you time and calories. Remember to marinate the chicken for 24 hours before proceeding with the recipe.

Ingredients:

For the chicken:

2 pounds skinless boneless chicken breast (sliced into long 1/2-inch pieces)

1 teaspoon salt

1 teaspoon freshly ground pepper

Dash of chili powder

1 teaspoon nutmeg

1 teaspoon allspice

1 teaspoon sumac[*]

---

[*]   See "Where to Buy Guide" for purchasing information.

Juice and zest of 1 lemon
1/8 cup white vinegar
1/4 cup corn oil
5 garlic cloves, chopped
2 medium onions, chopped
For the tahini sauce:
1/4 cup tahini (sesame paste)
1 teaspoon lemon juice
Dash of chili powder
To serve:
1 package mini or regular pita bread
Hot sauce, for garnish, if desired
Assorted pickles or preserved lemons

Preparation:

Combine chicken slices, salt, freshly ground pepper, chili powder, nutmeg, allspice, sumac, lemon juice and zest, white vinegar, corn oil, garlic cloves, and onion in a large shallow bowl or dish. Stir to mix well and coat chicken. Cover with aluminum foil and place in refrigerator for 24 hours.

To make the tahini sauce, combine the tahini and lemon juice in a medium bowl and mix well. Add enough water to thin the sauce to a syrupy consistency. Stir in chili powder. Taste and add salt and pepper if necessary. Cover and store in refrigerator until needed.

After chicken has marinated for 24 hours, preheat oven to 425°F.

Remove chicken from refrigerator and drain well. Spread chicken in a single layer on a baking sheet. Bake in the lower half of the oven for 25 minutes, turning once. Taste chicken and adjust seasonings if necessary.

Cut pitas in half. Place on a baking sheet and heat to warm in the oven, 1 to 2 minutes.

Remove pitas from oven and top with chicken meat. Serve on a platter with small bowls of hot sauce, tahini sauce, and pickles or preserved lemons.

Serves 4.

Mini Lamb Pita Sandwiches
(Shwarma bil Lahma Dani)

This is a lamb version of the pita sandwiches in the previous recipe. Restaurant rotisseries slowly roast meats, allowing restaurants to serve inexpensive cuts. For home cooking, it's best to use a more expensive cut of meat to compensate for the quick cooking time. Keep in mind that lamb needs to be marinated 24 hours.

Ingredients:
2 pounds lamb filet, sliced into thin 1/2-inch strips
1 onion, chopped
5 garlic cloves, chopped
2 tablespoons Saudi Spice Mix (see page 3)
Juice and peel of 1 lemon
1/4 cup white vinegar
1/4 cup corn oil
2 tablespoons clarified butter (ghee)
2 large tomatoes, sliced
1 package mini or regular pitas

Preparation:
Place lamb, onion, garlic, Saudi Spice Mix, lemon juice, lemon peel, vinegar, and corn oil in a large, shallow dish. Turn well to coat meat. Cover and refrigerate for 24 hours.

After lamb has finished marinating, preheat oven to 425°F.

Remove cover from lamb and drain well. Spread lamb in a single layer on a baking sheet. Top with tomato slices and dab clarified butter around meat. Bake for 30 minutes, turning once, until lamb is cooked through and tender.

Cut pitas in half. Place on a baking sheet and heat to warm in the oven, 1 to 2 minutes. Remove pitas from oven and top with lamb and tomato slices. Serve warm.

Serves 4.

Saudi Spiced Prawns
(Jamberi Saudi)

You can never serve enough of these scrumptious shrimp when entertaining. They disappear in minutes!

Ingredients:

1 cup plain dry breadcrumbs
1 tablespoon Saudi Spice Mix (see page 3)
Zest of 1 orange
2 large eggs, beaten
2 pounds large shrimp, peeled and deveined
2 cups corn or canola oil for frying
Salt, to taste

Preparation:

Combine breadcrumbs, Saudi Spice Mix, and orange zest in
a shallow bowl. Pour eggs into another shallow bowl.
Dip shrimp into eggs, shake off excess, and dip in
breadcrumbs to coat. Set on a platter. Repeat until all
shrimp are breaded.

Heat corn or canola oil in a large frying pan over medium
heat. Fry shrimp for about 5 minutes per side, or until
golden and cooked through.

Season with salt and serve hot.
Serves 4.

***Tip: You can serve this dish with French fries and salad for
dinner on a busy weeknight.***

Roasted Red Pepper and Tomato Soup
(Hasaa Filfil Ahmar wa Tomatum)

This soup is garnished with *zataar* croutons and goat cheese.
Try serving it in clear, heatproof cylindrical glasses for a stylish
presentation.

Ingredients:

For the soup:
1 (12-ounce) jar fire-roasted peppers, drained
4 cups chicken or vegetable stock
1 cup chopped tomatoes
2 cloves garlic, chopped
Salt, to taste
Freshly ground pepper, to taste
1/4 cup whipping cream

For the zataar *croutons:*
4 tablespoons olive oil
1 pita, cut into 1-inch pieces
1/4 cup *Zataar* Spice Mix (see page 64)
6 teaspoons goat cheese, for garnish

Preparation:
Combine peppers, stock, tomatoes, garlic, salt, and freshly
ground pepper in a medium saucepan. Bring to a boil
over high heat and stir to mix well. Reduce heat to low,
cover, and simmer for 20 minutes.

Remove from heat, stir, and pour into blender. Puree in
blender until smooth and pour back into saucepan. Stir
in cream and simmer, on low, until serving. Taste and
adjust salt if necessary.

To make the croutons, preheat broiler. Brush olive oil onto
pita pieces and place on a baking sheet. Top with *Zataar*
Spice Mix. Place under broiler and toast until golden, 1
to 2 minutes on each side.

Pour soup into serving cups or bowls. Top with *zataar* croutons and a piece of goat cheese. Serve hot.
Serves 4 to 6.

**Tip: Soup can be made ahead of time and stored in the refrig-
erator. Reheat on low so that cream doesn't curdle.**

Sunset Cocktail
(Cocktail Aghrub Ashams)
This cocktail is a tropical feast in a glass.

Ingredients:
1 cup mango juice, chilled
1 cup guava juice, chilled
1 cup papaya juice, chilled
1 cup unsweetened pineapple juice, chilled
1 banana, sliced
Fresh pineapple chunks, for garnish

Preparation:
Combine mango juice, guava juice, papaya juice, pineapple

juice, and banana in a blender. Puree until smooth. Pour
into serving glasses. Place 1 or 2 pineapple chunks on
the rim of each glass. Serve immediately.
Serves 4 to 6.

Red Sky Cocktail (*Cocktail Asama'Hamra'a*)
I drank this sweet sensation in Medina, Saudi Arabia. Fruit
"kabobs" were used as a garnish.

Ingredients:
1 1/2 cups blueberry
syrup
1 cup strawberry
syrup
1 cup orange juice
1 cup mango juice
1 cup peach juice
2 cups fresh fruit
chunks (strawberries,
melon, orange, apple,
or your favorite)
6 wooden skewers
(short to medium)

Preparation:
Combine blueberry
syrup, strawberry
syrup, orange juice,
mango juice, and
peach juice in
blender. Puree un-
til smooth. Pour
into glasses.

Skewer fruit onto wooden skewers. Be sure to leave the bottom half of the skewer, which will be in the drink, bare
and fill only the top portion with fruit.
Serves 6.

**Tip: Make fruit skewers the night before and store in the
refrigerator.**

Kiwi Cocktail
(Cocktail bil Kiwi)

Kiwis are native to China. To English speakers they were originally known as Chinese gooseberries. Kiwis contain vitamins C and K, as well as folate and potassium. They are available in gold, green, and baby varieties.

Ingredients:
5 green kiwis, sliced, divided
2 cups unsweetened pineapple juice, chilled
2 bananas, sliced
4 teaspoons honey
Ice, if desired

Preparation:
Place 4 sliced kiwis, pineapple juice, bananas, and honey in
  blender. Puree for 2 minutes or until smooth. Pour into
  glasses. Garnish with remaining kiwi slices. Serve immediately, over ice if desired.
Serves 4.

Almond Baklava
(Ba'lawa bil Lowz)

Orange and almonds combine to lend a light, fragrant taste to this classic dessert.

Ingredients:
For the syrup:
1 1/2 cups sugar
2 large strips of orange peel
Juice of 1 small orange
For the filling:
1 1/2 cups blanched almonds
1/2 cup sugar
1 teaspoon orange blossom water
For the baklava:
1 (1-pound) package phyllo dough, thawed according to package instructions
1 cup clarified butter (ghee)

Preparation:

Preheat oven to 350°F. Butter a 11x17-inch or 12-inch round baking pan.

To make the syrup, combine sugar, 1 cup water, zest, and juice in a medium saucepan. Bring to a boil over medium heat and stir until sugar dissolves. Discontinue stirring and reduce heat to low. Simmer for 10 minutes and set aside to cool. Remove orange peel and discard.

To make the filling, combine almonds, sugar, and orange blossom water in a food processor. Pulse until almonds are finely chopped. Pour into a bowl and set aside.

To assemble the baklava, remove phyllo dough from package. Trim it with a sharp knife to fit the pan you are using. Wrap excess dough in plastic wrap in the refrigerator.

Cover bottom of baking pan with 1 sheet of phyllo dough. Brush clarified butter over the top. Stack another sheet over the top. Brush with more clarified butter. Continue stacking and brushing with butter until half of the phyllo dough is used. Spread filling evenly across the top. Continue layering remaining phyllo dough and brushing with clarified butter. Brush top layer with clarified butter.

With a long, sharp knife, cut phyllo into 10 strips horizontally, being careful to cut only 3/4 of the way down, not all the way through the phyllo. Cut diagonal lines across the strips, again cutting only 3/4 of the way down, to create diamonds.

Bake for 40 to 50 minutes total, or until golden. Rotate pan every 20 minutes to ensure even browning. Remove pan from oven and pour syrup over the top. Allow to sit until syrup is absorbed and baklava has cooled to room temperature.

Serves 15 to 20.

Tip: You can tell when the syrup is ready by looking at the orange zest strips.
When the strips start to resemble candied orange peel, the syrup is at the right consistency.

Entertaining Timeline

One month to one week before the party:
Invite guests.

Buy spices and spice jars for Saudi Spice Mix (see page 3) favor.

Fill jars with spice mix.

Make syrup for Almond Baklava and refrigerate.

Confirm the number of guests and make grocery list accordingly.

Buy Arabic pop music, if desired.

Order centerpiece, or plan to make one.

Two days before the party:
Buy groceries.

Marinate the chicken for Mini Chicken Pita Sandwiches.

Marinate the lamb for Mini Lamb Pita Sandwiches.

Pick up or make centerpiece.

One day before the party:
Make Red Lentil Dip without garnish and refrigerate.

Bake chicken and lamb (separately) for sandwiches. Cool and refrigerate meat.

Make Roasted Red Pepper and Tomato Soup without *zataar* croutons and refrigerate.

Make Almond Baklava and refrigerate.

Prepare garnishes for cocktails.

Day of the Party:
Remove Almond Baklava from refrigerator and bring to room temperature.

Arrange Almond Baklava on a serving platter or cake plate.

Make *zataar* croutons for soup.

Make Sunset, Red Sky, and Kiwi Cocktails.

Make Saudi Spiced Prawns.

Reheat Red Lentil Dip, garnish, and serve.

Reheat Roasted Red Pepper Soup, garnish, and serve.

CHAPTER 12
Children's Pearl Diving Party

Until the 1930s pearl diving was a common occupation among Bahrainis. When the pearl industry crashed, many men had to find other occupations. Their love of the sea, however, never diminished. Diving is now an extremely popular sport not only in Bahrain but throughout the entire Arabian Peninsula. Many diving clubs and centers exist along the coastal areas.

This party, although fun for anyone, seems to be particularly suited to children. It's a great way to get children interested in other cultures, and many games could be planned around the pearl-diving theme. It could be a costume party for which children dress up in beach- or diving-inspired costumes. When they arrive at the party, each child should receive a strand of pearls and be welcomed to the Arabian Peninsula. Party placemats can be made from maps of the Arabian Peninsula or from pictures of ocean life magnified to fit a standard sheet of paper. If the children enjoy cooking, plan on making one or two of the recipes with them. Don't forget to let the kids frost their own biscuits with marshmallow topping.

After they are welcomed and fed, the children should be escorted to an inflatable pool or bathtub filled with seashells, some with (fake) pearls and some without. They can "hunt" for the pearls, and whoever finds the most wins a prize. Explain to the children where pearls actually come from. By the end of the party the children will have tasted new flavors, learned about the origins of pearls, and thus been exposed to another part of the world.

Menu
Salad:
Cilantro Salad in Endive "Boats" (*Salata Ducos*)
Main Courses:
Rice with Date Molasses (*Roz Muhammar*)

Fish and Rice Skillet (*Machbous bil Samak*)
Prawns in Tomato Sauce (*Jamberi bil Masala*)
Drink:
Grenadine Cocktail (*Cocktail Ahmar*)
Dessert:
Crunchy Pistachio-Filled Biscuits with Marshmallow
Topping (*Karabish*)
Favor:
Pearl Strands

Cilantro Salad in Endive "Boats" (*Salata Ducos*)

This is a delicious and healthful salad that even children
can be enticed to eat. If you serve it in individual leaves, it can be
picked up and eaten with the fingers.

Ingredients:
1 tablespoon olive oil
Juice of 2 lemons
Salt, to taste
Freshly ground pepper, to taste
1 bunch cilantro, finely chopped
2 medium tomatoes, diced
2 heads endive

Preparation:
Whisk the olive oil, lemon juice, salt, and pepper together in
a small bowl. Taste and adjust seasonings if necessary.
Set aside.
Place cilantro and tomatoes in a medium bowl and toss with
dressing to coat.
Cut the base off of the endive and remove the outer leaves.
Carefully remove each leaf so that it does not tear.
Fill the inside of the leaves with a few tablespoons of salad.
Set on a platter. Serve at room temperature.
Serves 4 to 6.

Rice with Date Molasses (*Roz Muhammar*)

In the nineteenth century, Qatar became a pearl-diving capital of the world. Pearl divers' diets were centered on carbohydrates

and sugar, which were necessary to maintain their high energy levels, and this recipe is said to have been one of their staples.

Ingredients:
1/2 teaspoon saffron, crushed
1 teaspoon ground cardamom
1 teaspoon ground cinnamon
1 tablespoon rose water
2 cups basmati rice, soaked in water for 20 minutes and drained
Salt, to taste
1/2 cup date molasses*
1 tablespoon clarified butter (ghee) or butter

Preparation:
In small bowl, mix saffron, cardamom, cinnamon, and rose water. Set aside.

In a large saucepan, bring 6 cups of water to a boil over high heat and add rice. Add salt to the rice, stir well, and cook, uncovered, over medium-low heat for 10 minutes. Drain the rice, pour it into a bowl and stir in the date molasses. Use a fork to fluff the rice and mix well.

Melt the clarified butter in a large saucepan over medium heat. Add the rice to the saucepan and stir well. Cover the pot with a clean kitchen cloth and then a lid. Cook over low heat for 20 minutes, or until rice is done. Taste rice and adjust seasonings if necessary.

Serves 4.

Fish and Rice Skillet (*Machbous bil Samak*)

Kuwait is located on the Arabian Sea, and thus its fisherman have always had access to a continuous supply of fresh fish and seafood. Its traders often brought back spices and influence from Pakistan and Western India as well. Recipes taking their inspiration from the Indian subcontinent have become part of modern Kuwaiti cuisine. *Machbous* is a dish made out of mutton,

---

*   See "Where to Buy Guide" for purchasing information.

chicken, or fish served over fragrant rice. It is closely related to Indian *biryani*. This version is made with fish fillets. Any white fish like tilapia, cod, sole, or haddock will work well with this dish.

Ingredients:
1 tablespoon clarified butter (ghee)
1 onion, diced
3 garlic cloves, minced
1 1/2 pounds boneless fish fillets
1 teaspoon *garam masala**
1 teaspoon turmeric
1 cup tomato puree
1 teaspoon salt
1 cup basmati rice, soaked in water for 20 minutes, rinsed, and drained

Preparation:
Heat clarified butter in a large saucepan over medium heat. Add onion, stir, and sauté until translucent, about 3 to 5 minutes. Stir in garlic. Add fish fillets, *garam masala*, and turmeric, and cook fish 3 to 5 minutes per side until opaque. Add tomato puree and 1 cup water. Stir gently around the fish to combine.

Season with 1 teaspoon salt and add rice in between the pieces of fish. Stir rice and sauce together to combine. Increase heat to high and bring to a boil. Reduce heat to low, cover tightly, and simmer for 20 to 30 minutes, or until rice is tender and fish is cooked through. Taste and adjust seasonings if necessary.

Remove from heat, keep covered, and let sit for 5 to 10 minutes before serving. Serve warm.

Serves 4.

Prawns in Tomato Sauce (Jamberi bil Masala)
Once called "prawn masala" by the Indians who introduced it to the Arabian Peninsula, Prawns in Tomato Sauce quickly

----

* See "Where to Buy Guide" for purchasing information.

became a favorite of Bahrainis. Many variations of this dish exist, and it is always served with rice.

Ingredients:
1 tablespoon corn oil
1 green chili pepper, chopped
2 cups chopped tomatoes
1 teaspoon salt
3 tablespoons tomato paste
1 teaspoon fresh ginger, grated
1 teaspoon chili powder
1 teaspoon ground coriander
1/2 teaspoon *garam masala*
2 pounds fresh prawns, peeled and deveined

Preparation:
Heat oil in a large saucepan over medium heat. Add green peppers, tomatoes, salt, tomato paste, ginger, chili powder, coriander, and *garam masala*. Stir in 3/4 cup water and bring to a boil, uncovered. Add prawns to the sauce, stir, and reduce heat to low. Simmer 15 to 20 minutes, covered, until shrimp are cooked through. Serve warm.
Serves 6.

Grenadine Cocktail (*Cocktail Ahmar*)
Kids love the color and taste of this drink.

Ingredients:
4 cups cold water
Juice of 1 lemon
4 tablespoons grenadine
1 cup sugar
Maraschino cherries, for garnish

Preparation:
Stir water, lemon juice, grenadine, and sugar together in a pitcher. Pour into clear glasses and top with maraschino cherries.
Serves 4.

Crunchy Pistachio-Filled Biscuits with Marshmallow Topping (Karabish)

These biscuits have a unique crunchy exterior made by combining cream of wheat and flour. In addition to its delicious taste, this dough also offers beauty benefits. The clarified butter, cream of wheat, and semolina combine to make a wonderful exfoliant and moisturizer for the skin. After working with the dough, do not wash your hands with soap. "Work" the leftover dough into your hands for a few minutes, and rinse with warm water. You're hands will be soft and smooth for days!

The topping for the biscuit is traditionally made from *halawa* root and worked into a sweet fluff called *natef*. This topping is usually bought ready-made at Arabian bakeries. In the United States, marshmallow fluff is often substituted. If preparing these biscuits for a children's party, allow the children to "frost" their own cookies with the marshmallow fluff.

Ingredients:
For the cookies:
4 cups uncooked cream of wheat (*farina*)
1 cup semolina*
1 cup sugar
1 pound clarified butter (ghee)
1 teaspoon *mahlab*
1 teaspoon active dry yeast
For the topping:
1 jar marshmallow fluff
For the filling:
1 cup shelled pistachios
1 teaspoon ground cardamom
1 tablespoon sugar
1 teaspoon orange blossom water
1 teaspoon rose water

---

*   See "Where to Buy Guide" for purchasing information for semolina and *mahlab*.

Preparation:

In a large bowl, combine cream of wheat, semolina, sugar, clarified butter, *mahlab*, and yeast. Cover and let sit out overnight.

In the morning, knead the dough and set it aside to rest for 30 minutes.

Preheat oven to 375°F. Line 2 baking sheets with parchment paper or silicone mats.

Combine pistachios, cardamom, sugar, 1 tablespoon water, orange blossom water, and rose water in the bowl of a food processor. Pulse until pistachios are coarsely ground and all ingredients are combined. Set 1/4 cup of mixture aside for garnish.

Fill a shallow bowl with water for wetting your fingers. After dough has rested, knead again, and with wet fingers, divide dough into golf-ball-size pieces. Dip one of your palms in water and flatten a ball of dough with it. Place 1 scant teaspoon filling in the middle of the dough circle. Wet the other hand and close the circle over the filling. Shape filled dough into oblong logs approximately 3-inches long by 1-inch wide. Place logs 1 inch apart on prepared cookie sheets.

Bake for 20 to 25 minutes, or until golden. Remove from oven and let cool in pans. Cool completely and then top each cookie with 1 tablespoon of fluff. Garnish with a few leftover pistachio pieces.

Makes 2 1/2 dozen.

Tip: Top cookies with fluff immediately before serving so that the fluff doesn't melt.

Entertaining Timeline

One month to one week before the event:
Invite guests.

Call parents to make sure their children have no dietary restrictions or concerns and adjust menu if necessary.

Confirm the number of guests and make grocery list accordingly.

Buy pearl favors.

Buy seashells, fake pearls, and any other necessary items for the pearl-diving game.

Two days before the event:
Buy groceries.

Make the dough for the Crunchy Pistachio-Filled Biscuits.

Make Grenadine Cocktail and refrigerate.

One day before the event:
Make Crunchy Pistachio-Filled Biscuits.

Make Prawns in Tomato Sauce and store in refrigerator.

Set table.

Set up games and "diving" station.

Day of the event:
Make Fish and Rice Skillet.

Make Rice with Date Molasses.

Make Cilantro Salad in Endive "Boats" and reheat Prawns in Tomato Sauce.

CHAPTER 13
Bedouin Desert Truffle Party

The illusive desert truffle is one of the best-kept secrets of the Middle East. A truffle is a mushroom belonging to the tuber species. Truffles are different from other mushrooms because they have a symbiotic relationship with trees. Most of the truffles eaten in antiquity were Arabic desert truffles. They were the fare of Bedouins, kings, emperors, and pharaohs alike.

Nowadays, desert truffles grow across North Africa and into the Arabian Peninsula, through Syria, Lebanon, Iraq, and Israel. Many people are amazed that these truffles grow in the desert, where there are no trees for them to depend on. In fact, the desert truffles grow in symbiosis with a member of the rock rose family called the rag-rug plant.

Black Desert Truffles

The truffles receive nutrients from the rag-rug through filaments that penetrate the roots of the plant. In return, the truffles produce a substance that inhibits the growth of plants that could harm the rag-rug plants.

Bedouins attest that desert truffles grow in collaboration

with thunder. When lightning splits the earth, they appear. Without the forces of lightning and thunder, no truffles emerge. Without storms, truffle hunters may go as many as five years without seeing a truffle. The cost of the desert truffle is much less than that of European truffles because they grow in such large quantities. In the last five years, desert truffles have sold for between $13 and $130 per pound, depending upon the supply.

Arabic desert truffles are the main component of many traditional Bedouin recipes. They can be eaten raw or cooked. In Kuwait, they are boiled in camel's milk or roasted in clarified butter. Truffles are often exported to the United Arab Emirates and Saudi Arabia for sale. In Saudi Arabia, King Abdullah includes desert truffles on his menu when entertaining heads of state. Saudi Arabia is known for its *khalasi* variety, which is black skinned with a pink interior, and the cream-colored *zubaydi* variety.

Desert truffles are prized by Bedouins for their medicinal and spiritual values. They are considered both a blessing and a cure for eye ailments. The Prophet Muhammad said, "Truffles are the manna of manna, and their water contains a cure for the eyes." According to Imam Muhammad Al-Akili in *Nature Healing with the Medicine of the Prophet*, this saying has been interpreted to mean that truffles are a gift from the heavens because they require no work to cultivate. The word *manna* in this saying is the Arabic verb meaning "favor," referring to one of the favors that God bestowed on the Children of Israel in the form of food. Bedouins use truffle water to cure their eyes from infection and to treat night blindness and burning of the eyes.

The menu for this party celebrates the desert truffle. This party is casual and should be held outdoors, if possible. Use brightly patterned fabrics to set up "tents" and serve the food picnic-style on plastic tablecloths on the ground. Dishes should be served in the same pots and pans that they are prepared in. The favor for this party is a special blend of Bedouin tea. See the "Where to Buy Guide" for purchasing information for desert truffles. When the supply of truffles is scarce, it can be difficult to find them in the United States, so I've included substitutions for the truffles with each recipe.

Menu
Salad:
Mixed Salad with Lime Dressing (*Salata Khadra bil Lamoon*)
Main Courses:
Khaleeji White Rice (*Roz Khaleeji*)

Oven-Roasted Lamb with Saffron and Truffles (*Fag'gah bil Lahma*)

Beef and Cracked Wheat Stew (*Jarrish bil Lahma*)
Drink:
Bedouin Tea (*Shai Bedawi*)
Dessert:
"Desert Truffle" Cookies (*Biskoweet "Fag'gah Aswad"*)

Dates (purchased)
Favor:
Bedouin Tea bags

Mixed Salad with Lime Dressing (*Salata Khadra bil Lamoon*)

Limes are a common ingredient in salad dressing in the Arabian Peninsula. You may substitute other fresh vegetables and herbs for the ones listed below.

Ingredients:
1 bunch cilantro, finely chopped

1 bunch flat-leaf parsley, finely chopped

1 green pepper, diced

1 large tomato, diced

1/4 cup olive or corn oil

Zest and juice of 3 limes

Salt, to taste

Freshly ground pepper, to taste

Dash of cumin

Dash of chili powder

1/2 teaspoon sugar, if needed

Preparation:
Place cilantro, parsley, green pepper, and tomato in a large bowl.

Whisk olive oil, lime zest, lime juice, salt, pepper, cumin, and chili powder together in a medium bowl. Taste dressing and add sugar if needed.

Pour dressing over salad and toss to combine.

Serves 4.

Tip: Prepare salad and dressing a day ahead of time and store, separately, in the refrigerator. Toss to combine just before serving.

Khaleeji White Rice (Roz Khaleeji)

This white rice recipe can be enjoyed anytime.

Ingredients:

1 cup basmati rice
1 teaspoon clarified butter (ghee) or unsalted butter
1 teaspoon salt

Preparation:

Soak basmati rice in water for 20 minutes and drain. Combine rice, clarified butter or butter, salt, and 1 3/4 cup water in a medium saucepan. Bring to a boil on high heat, stir, reduce heat to low, cover, and simmer for 15 minutes, or until all liquid is absorbed. Remove from heat and let stand for 5 to 10 minutes. Fluff with a fork and serve hot.

Serves 4.

Tip: Use 1 cup leftover rice to make Chicken Stuffed with Rice and Meat (see page 92).

Oven-Roasted Lamb with Saffron and Truffles (Fag'gah bil Lahma)

At the time of this book's publication, Arabic desert truffles were difficult to find in the United States. The countries that produce them must distribute them to their own consumers before they export them to other countries in the Arabian Peninsula, which have a large demand for them. In years when the truffles are scarce, it is virtually impossible to get them in the

United States. I've decided to include this recipe anyway, in anticipation that next year's truffle harvest will be more bountiful. If necessary, you can substitute potatoes, rutabagas, turnips, artichokes, or fennel for the desert truffles.

Ingredients:
1 tablespoon corn oil
3 onions, thinly sliced
6 lamb shanks
1 teaspoon high-quality saffron
1 teaspoon turmeric
Salt, to taste
Freshly ground pepper, to taste
4 pounds Arabic truffles, peeled and sliced into 2-inch chunks[*]

Preparation:
Preheat oven to 425°F.
Heat oil in a large, ovenproof saucepan. Add onions and sauté on medium heat until brown, 5 to 7 minutes. Add lamb and brown on all sides, 10 minutes. Season lamb with saffron, turmeric, and salt and pepper. Turn meat to coat. Pour enough water over lamb to barely cover and place in the oven, uncovered. Roast for 1 1/2 hours, turning every half an hour.
Add sliced truffles or vegetables and mix in remaining liquid. Add more water to cover if necessary.
Bake for another 30 minutes, or until lamb, truffles, and vegetables are tender. Serve warm.
Serves 4 to 6.

Beef and Cracked Wheat Stew
(Jarrish bi Lahma)
I first sampled this dish at the guest palace in Jeddah, Saudi Arabia. It has a very delicate and soothing taste.

---

[*]   Sold in cans in Arabic stores when available.

Ingredients:
1 tablespoon corn oil
1 onion, diced
1 pound boneless beef shoulder, cubed
2 cups chicken or meat stock
1 cup tomato puree
Salt, to taste
Freshly ground pepper, to taste
2 cinnamon sticks
1 cup cracked wheat*

Preparation:
Heat corn oil in a large saucepan over medium heat. Add onion and sauté until soft, about 3 to 5 minutes. Add meat and brown on all sides. Add stock, tomato puree, salt, freshly ground pepper, and cinnamon. Mix to combine well. Add cracked wheat and stir again. Increase heat to high and bring to a boil. Reduce heat to low and simmer, covered, with the lid slightly ajar, for 1 1/2 hours until meat and cracked wheat are tender. If liquid evaporates before cooking time is up, add more water or stock, and continue simmering until meat and cracked wheat are tender.

Remove cinnamon sticks. Serve warm.
Serves 4.

Bedouin Tea
(Shai Bedawi)
Bedouins make special blends of teas from the dried leaves of various desert plants. On special occasions, they mix the leaves from those plants with other spices. This recipe contains Bedouin tea, dried rosebuds, cinnamon, and black tea. Bedouin tea is available in the Middle East at spice shops in areas that have a significant Bedouin population. It is quite expensive because it is scarce. In the United States, dried thyme or sage can be substituted for the Bedouin tea.

---

*   See "Where to Buy Guide" for purchasing information.

Ingredients:
4 teaspoons Bedouin tea, dried thyme, or dried sage
4 teaspoons dried organic rosebuds
1 cinnamon stick
4 teaspoons loose black tea (regular or decaffeinated)
Sugar, if desired

Preparation:
Heat 4 1/2 cups water, Bedouin tea, dried rosebuds, cinnamon stick, and loose black tea in a teapot or saucepan over high heat. Once the water boils, reduce heat to low and simmer for 5 minutes. Turn off heat and steep tea, covered, for 5 minutes. Strain into teacups and sweeten with sugar, if desired.
Serves 4.

Tip: Make extra batches of this tea and place it in favor bags or small cheesecloth sachets to give to your guests as favors.

"Desert Truffle" Cookies (*Biskoweet "Fag'gah Aswad"*)
I came up with the idea for this recipe after watching an Iranian pastry chef, who operates a bakery in Dubai, United Arab Emirates, make a white "mushroom" cookie. I decided to use a similar dough and add cocoa, cardamom, and sugar on the exterior to mimic a desert truffle instead of a mushroom. These cookies taste great and are fun to bake with children.

Ingredients:
4 cups unbleached, all-purpose flour
1 1/2 cups organic vegetable shortening
1 1/2 cups confectioners' sugar
1 cup blanched almonds, ground to flour consistency in a
    food processor with a teaspoon of sugar
1 teaspoon vanilla
1/8 cup plus 1 teaspoon ground cardamom, divided
1/2 cup Dutch process cocoa, divided
1/4 cup granulated sugar

Preparation:

Preheat oven to 300°F. Line 3 baking sheets with parchment paper or silicone pats.

Mix flour, shortening, confectioners' sugar, ground almonds, vanilla, 1 teaspoon cardamom, and 1/4 cup of the cocoa together in a large bowl or in the bowl of an electric mixer. Mix by hand with a wooden spoon or with a mixer on low speed until all ingredients are combined to form dough.

Shape dough into a ball and place on a work surface. Shape dough into 1-inch balls.

Pour the remaining 1/4 cup of cocoa, 1/8 cup cardamom, and sugar onto 3 small, separate plates. Roll each ball in cocoa, then cardamom, and finally sugar, to coat. Rub the ball between your hands to incorporate the flavors. Place the balls on the prepared cookie sheets 1 inch apart.

Bake for 15 to 20 minutes, or until set. Cool on baking sheets. Transfer to a serving platter when cool.

Makes 4 dozen.

Note: Extra cookies can be stored in the freezer for up to 1 month.

Entertaining Timeline

One month to one week in advance:
Invite guests.

Purchase or organize outdoor tents and tablecloths.

Buy ingredients for Bedouin Tea.

Mix Bedouin Tea. Make enough for party and for each guest to take 1 recipe home as a favor.

Buy clear treat bags from a craft store and place tea inside bags as a favor to each guest.

Make grocery list and adjust ingredient quantities to reflect number of guests, if necessary.

Order desert truffles, if possible.

Make "Desert Truffle" Cookies and freeze.

Three days before the party:
Buy groceries.

One day before the party:
Set up tents outside, if possible.

Make Oven-Roasted Lamb with Saffron and Truffles and refrigerate.

Make Beef and Cracked Wheat Stew and refrigerate.

Day of the party:
Remove cookies from freezer to thaw.

Make *Khaleeji* White Rice.

Make Mixed Salad with Lime Dressing.

Reheat lamb and beef dishes.

Brew Bedouin Tea as guests arrive.

CHAPTER 14

Jeddah Red Sea Picnic

When I think of Jeddah, Saudi Arabia, the word "family" comes to mind. Jeddah is one of the most family-friendly places on earth. The city boasts many beautiful parks, marinas, shopping malls, and entertainment centers perfect for adults and children alike. The balmy weather, beautiful seashore, and wide, clean boulevards add to its appeal. Jeddah is an old port city, where ancient traditions and modern cosmopolitanism coexist.

After the opening of the Suez Canal in 1869, the trade industry began to thrive in Jeddah. During the period after the canal opening, houses in the old quarter of Jeddah were built of coral stone from nearby quarries. Dates were ground into pulp and made into mortar to hold the stones together.

Red Sea Marina, Jeddah, Saudi Arabia

Although the city is extremely beautiful in the daytime, the nighttime in Jeddah is magical. For starters, a huge fountain shaped like an incense censor lights up in the Red Sea and water shoots out of it as if it were the smoke from incense. Jeddah's main boulevards are dotted with enormous modern sculptures, which are lit up at night. People stroll along the *corniche* (seaside street) and converse with one another.

Friday nights are picnic nights for families along the Red Sea banks. Picnickers line the banks with Persian carpets and folding lawn chairs, which they bring with them, and then, set up transistor radios and boom boxes and, nowadays, portable TVs. Thermoses full of Arabic coffee and plentiful fish and rice dishes are served. The talking, feasting, and relaxing go on for hours.

If possible, try to plan this party as an outdoor, evening picnic. If the parks in your area close early, you may need to set up the picnic in your backyard or at a local lake. There is something peaceful about being outdoors in the evening. Be sure to stock your car like the Saudis do: with something to sit on, music, and, of course, delicious food. This menu is inspired by the sea. Seafood enthusiasts will love it.

Menu

Appetizer:
   Fish and Potato Croquettes (*Koftat Samak*)
Soup:
   Arabian Calamari Soup (*Hasaa Calamari*)
Salad:
   Mixed Herb Plate (*Salata Bassal wa Khodar*)
Main Course:
   Fish with Tamarind Glaze (*Samak bil Tamr Hindi*)
Drink:
   Arabic Cardamom Coffee (see page 101)
Dessert:
   Date, Almond, and Sesame Balls (*Tamr bil Lowz wa SimSim*)

Fish and Potato Croquettes (*Koftat Samak*)

Fish and Potato Croquettes are wonderful snacks and appetizers. They can also be served with soup and salad for lunch or dinner. They are best served hot, moments after they are made.

Ingredients:

1 pound russet potatoes, scrubbed, peeled, and cubed
1 pound boneless sole or cod fillets, chopped into 1-inch pieces
4 cups plus 2 tablespoons corn oil, divided
2 tablespoons flour
4 garlic cloves, chopped
3 tablespoons fresh parsley, chopped

Fish and Potato Croquettes

1/2 cup plain dry breadcrumbs
2 large eggs, lightly beaten
Salt, to taste
Freshly ground pepper, to taste
2 limes, sliced

Preparation:

Place potatoes in a large, heavy saucepan and cover with water. Bring to a boil on high heat and then reduce heat to medium. Cook, uncovered, for 15 to 20 minutes, or until potatoes are fork tender. Drain and place in a bowl of cold water for 5 minutes to stop cooking. Drain again and reserve.

Place potatoes, fish pieces, 2 tablespoons corn oil, flour, garlic cloves, and parsley in a food processor and mix until a smooth paste forms. Form golf-ball-size pieces of dough into balls or egg shapes. If mixture is too sticky to work with, add more flour, a tablespoon at a time, until it becomes easy to handle. Place balls on a large platter. Continue shaping croquettes until all dough is used. Refrigerate croquettes for 30 minutes.

About 5 minutes before you remove croquettes from refrigerator, heat 4 cups of corn oil in a large, heavy frying pan over medium heat. Pour breadcrumbs onto a plate. Pour eggs into a shallow bowl and whisk until combined. Remove croquettes from refrigerator and dip into beaten eggs, shake off excess, and coat in breadcrumbs. Set on another platter.

When oil reaches 300°F, begin frying croquettes: Lower them into the pan, carefully, making sure to leave space between them. Fry for 5 minutes per side, or until golden and cooked through. Remove from oil and

transfer to a plate lined with paper towels.
Taste and season with salt and freshly ground pepper if
needed. Garnish with lime slices. Serve warm.
Serves 4 to 6.

*Tip: Wrap hot croquettes in aluminum foil to keep them
warm until serving time.*

Arabian Calamari Soup (*Hasaa Calamari*)

The simplicity of this fragrant soup will surprise calamari
lovers. For a picnic, be sure to pour the soup into a large thermos
while it is hot so that it remains warm until served. Keep in
mind that Saudi picnics usually take place on breezy evenings,
so warm soup is a necessity. I do not recommend serving the
soup on a hot summer day.

Ingredients:
1 tablespoon corn oil
1 onion, diced
1 tablespoon tomato paste
1 tablespoon fresh ginger, grated
4 garlic cloves, minced
1/2 cup tomatoes, chopped
1 teaspoon Saudi Spice Mix (see page 3)
1 dried lime*
2 1/2 pounds calamari, cleaned, heads and tentacles removed,
     cut into 1/4-inch rings
6 cups vegetable or fish stock
Salt, to taste

Preparation:
Heat corn oil in a medium stockpot over medium heat. Add
     onion and sauté until translucent, 3 to 5 minutes. Add
     tomato paste, ginger, garlic, tomato, spice mix, dried
     lime, and calamari. Stir to incorporate. Add stock and
     bring to a boil over high heat. Reduce heat to low, cover,

---

* See "Where to Buy Guide" for purchasing information.

and simmer for 20 minutes until vegetables and calamari are tender. Taste and adjust salt, if necessary. Serve hot.
Serves 4.

Tip: *Diced potatoes or zucchini can be added to the soup to make it a complete meal.*

Mixed Herb Plate (Salata Bassal wa Khodar)

Eating arugula with onions and fish is common in the Arabian Peninsula. Interestingly, arugula grows abundantly throughout the Mediterranean and Middle East. There, it is not seen as a gourmet food item but a staple like lettuce or parsley. The leaves are served whole and sometimes garnished with a bit of the cooking sauce from fish. Otherwise, they are eaten without condiment.

Ingredients:
1 bunch fresh arugula
2 bunches spring onions
1 bunch fresh parsley or dill, washed and dried

Preparation:
Immerse arugula in water in a large bowl. Drain and repeat until arugula is clean and no residue remains on bottom of the bowl (this may take as many as 7 washings). Dry arugula and lay it on a large serving platter.

Trim ends off of spring onions and lay them on top of arugula. Arrange parsley or dill next to spring onions.
Serves 4 to 6.

Tip: *Make herb plate in advance and refrigerate, covered, until needed.*

Fish with Tamarind Glaze (Samak bil Tamr Hindi)

The tamarind glaze gives this fish a sweet and sour taste. This recipe is extremely simple to make. Use whichever white fish you can find whole and in season. Rockfish works particularly well.

Ingredients:
1 teaspoon corn oil
1 large onion, diced
1 whole (3- to 4-pound) fish, cleaned
2 garlic cloves, minced
1/2 cup tamarind paste,* diluted in 2 cups of water
1 teaspoon Saudi Spice Mix (see page 3)
1 teaspoon salt
1 lime, sliced thinly

Preparation:
Preheat oil to 350°F.
Grease a large baking dish with corn oil and add onion to the bottom of the pan. Place fish on top of onions. Place some of the onions and garlic inside fish cavity. Cover fish with tamarind paste. Sprinkle with Saudi Spice Mix and salt. Cover with aluminum foil and bake for 1 hour, or until fish is cooked and flakes easily when cut. Transfer to a serving platter. Garnish with lime slices.
Serves 4 to 6.

Tip: To cut down on cooking time, use fish fillets instead of whole fish and bake for 20 minutes. Add sliced vegetables to the pan during baking to make a complete meal.

Date, Almond, and Sesame Balls
(Tamr bil Lowz wa SimSim)
I like to call these sweet treats healthful bonbons. They have the look of an elegant chocolate truffle but are packed with the nutritious properties of dates, almonds, and sesame seeds. For a quick energy boost, they're a great alternative to sugary sweets and candy. Since they require no baking, they're a wonderful beginner recipe for young children. Make Date, Almond, and Sesame Balls in advance and store in the refrigerator for up to a week or in the freezer for up to 1 month.

---

* See "Where to Buy Guide" for purchasing information.

Ingredients:

1 pound soft dates, pitted
1/4 cup butter, at room temperature
1/2 teaspoon rose water
1/2 teaspoon orange blossom water
1/2 pound blanched almonds
1 teaspoon ground cardamom
1/2 teaspoon ground cinnamon
1 cup sesame seeds, toasted

Preparation:

Place dates, butter, 1/4 cup water, rose water, orange blossom water, almonds, cardamom, and cinnamon in a food
processor. Pulse to form a smooth paste. Shape dough
into date-size balls. Spread sesame seeds on a baking
sheet. Roll date balls into sesame seeds to coat. Arrange
on a serving platter.
Makes 3 dozen.

Entertaining Timeline

One week before the picnic:
Invite friends.
Confirm guest list and adjust recipe quantities to reflect the number of guests, if necessary.
Make Date, Almond, and Sesame Balls.
Buy Arabic Cardamom Coffee, if necessary.*

Two days before the picnic:
Buy groceries.
Pack the car with tablecloth, chairs, and other supplies.

One day before the picnic:
Make Arabian Calamari Soup and refrigerate.
Make Fish with Tamarind Glaze and refrigerate.
Make Fish and Potato Croquettes and refrigerate.
Make Mixed Herb Plate and refrigerate.

Day of the picnic:
Pack plates, cups, napkins, and utensils.
Make Arabic Cardamom Coffee and store in thermos.
Reheat soup and store in thermos.
Reheat Fish with Tamarind Glaze and Fish and Potato Croquettes and wrap in aluminum foil.
Remove Mixed Herb Plate and Date, Almond, and Sesame Balls from refrigerator.

---

* See "Where to Buy Guide" for purchasing information.

CHAPTER 15
Oasis Date Harvest

Whole communities congregate to feast during the date harvest each fall. During the months of September, October, and November the branches of date palms are weighted down with ripe red and yellow dates. Fresh dates taste like a cross between an apple and a grape. They can be eaten alone, raw or used to create many delicious recipes.

In addition to having a sweet taste, dates are very nutritious. Since ancient times, dates have been used in the Arabian Peninsula to treat constipation, heart disease, anemia, and allergies, to prevent dizziness, to relieve heartburn and acid

Yellow dates

reflux, to stop multiplication of cancer cells, to stop bleeding during pregnancy, and to stimulate the reproductive system.

I've created this menu to showcase the versatility of the dried date. These recipes are straightforward and stress free, ideal for entertaining. The menu is perfect for a lovely family meal, birthday party, or picnic. Be sure to check that you can buy dates from your local supermarket before planning the party. Although dates are available almost all year round, they are much more plentiful around holiday time.

Decorate your table with a palm motif to signify date palms. Instead of displaying a traditional flower centerpiece, arrange baskets full of dates and place in the middle of each table.

Menu

Appetizer:
Basmati Rice with Dates and Apricots (*Roz bil Tamr wa Qamr Din*)

Salad:
Date, Orange, and Feta Ball Salad (*Salata bil Tamr, Bortuan, wa Jebna*)

Main Dish:
Cornish Hens Glazed with Date Molasses (*Cornish Hens bil Dabs al Tamr*)

Drink:
Date and Raisin Drink (*Jallab*)

Dessert:
Date and Walnut Cookies (*Biskoweet bil Tamr wa Jowza*)

Favor:
Assorted Dates

Basmati Rice with Dates and Apricots (*Roz bil Tamr wa Qamr Din*)

This fruity, fragrant rice is an excellent addition to anyone's repertoire.

Ingredients:
1 cup basmati rice, soaked in water for 20 minutes and rinsed
1/2 pound dates, pitted

1/4 cup dried apricots, chopped
2 whole cloves
2 green cardamom pods
1 teaspoon saffron
1 teaspoon salt
1 tablespoon unsalted butter

Preparation:
Place rice, dates, apricots, cloves, cardamom pods, saffron, and salt in a medium saucepan. Add 1 3/4 cup
water and stir. Add butter and bring to a boil over
high heat. Reduce heat to low, cover, and simmer for
20 minutes, or until tender. Taste and adjust salt, if
necessary.

Let stand, covered, for 10 minutes. Fluff rice with fork,
remove cardamom pods, and serve hot.
Serves 4.

Date, Orange, and Feta Ball Salad
(*Salata bil Tamr, Bortuan, wa Jebna*)
This is a bright and festive salad that can add flair to any
meal. I like to eat a large portion with bread as a meal.

Ingredients:
1 head romaine lettuce, chopped into 1-inch pieces
4 medium carrots, peeled and grated
1 (11-ounce) can mandarin oranges, rinsed
1/2 cup pitted dates
Juice of 1 orange
Juice of 1 lemon
1 teaspoon orange blossom water
Freshly ground pepper, to taste
1/2 cup feta cheese, drained
1 large egg
1/4 cup flour
Canola oil, for frying

Preparation:
Arrange romaine lettuce on the bottom of a large serving

dish. Scatter carrots on top of lettuce. Arrange mandarin oranges on top of carrots. Arrange pitted dates
around the top.

Make dressing by whisking orange juice, lemon juice, orange blossom water, and freshly ground pepper together
in a small bowl. Set aside.

Combine feta cheese, egg, and flour in a medium bowl. Using a fork or whisk, mix until light and fluffy.

Heat 2 inches of canola oil in a medium frying pan.

Roll feta mixture into 1-inch balls or use a melon baller to
make equal-size balls. Carefully drop feta balls into the
hot oil. Fry for 3 to 5 minutes per side, or until golden.
Remove with a slotted spoon and transfer to a platter
lined with paper towels. Arrange cheese on the top of
the salad.

Drizzle dressing over the salad. Serve immediately.

Serves 4 to 6.

Tip: *Goat cheese can be substituted for the feta cheese in this recipe.*

Cornish Hens Glazed with Date Molasses (Cornish Hens bil Dabs al Tamr)

Roasting meat with date molasses gives it a smoky, sweet, barbecue taste with a hint of date flavor. You can substitute a whole chicken for the four Cornish hens used in this recipe, if you prefer. Alternatively, you could grill chicken parts and slather them with date molasses before serving.

Ingredients:
1 tablespoon olive oil
4 Cornish hens, rinsed and dried
4 dried limes*
1/2 cup date molasses
2 teaspoons Omani Spice Mix (see page 130)
Salt, to taste

---

* See "Where to Buy Guide" for purchasing information.

Preparation:

Preheat oven to 425°F. Grease a 9x13-inch baking dish with olive oil.

Place Cornish hens in dish. Place a dried lime in the cavity of each one. Spoon date molasses over the top (backside) of the Cornish hens. Sprinkle each hen with 1/2 teaspoon Omani Spice Mix and salt. Cover with aluminum foil and bake for 1 1/2 hours or until juices from the thigh joint run clear when pierced, basting every 30 minutes with pan juices.

Remove from oven and let stand, covered, for 10 minutes. Baste again and serve warm.

Serves 4.

Date and Raisin Drink (Jallab)

This traditional drink is usually made with soaked raisins and grape molasses. I've replaced the grape molasses with date molasses to complement the date-themed menu. For an authentic touch, light an incense censor with your favorite loose incense and place the *Jallab* in a pitcher covered with a kitchen cloth next to the incense smoke. Allow the drink to absorb the incense aroma until the incense burns out. Keep in mind that the raisins need to be soaked overnight before you make the drink.

Ingredients:

1 cup raisins, stems removed, soaked overnight in 2 cups water
1/4 cup sugar, or to taste
1/2 cup date molasses
1 tablespoon rose water
1/2 cup dates, pitted and chopped, for garnish
1 cup crushed ice

Preparation:

Place raisins and soaking water, sugar, date molasses, and rose water in blender. Whip until all ingredients are combined. Place date pieces at the bottom of glasses. Distribute ice into each glass. Pour drink on top of ice. Serve immediately.

Serves 6.

Date and Walnut Cookies
(Biskoweet bil Tamr wa Jowz)

These buttery cookies are filled with a delicious date and almond paste, which used to be cooked for hours and pureed by hand. Nowadays, a food processor can do this job in minutes. These cookies can be made in advance and frozen. Because of the rolling involved, children love to assist in their preparation.

Ingredients:
For the filling:
1/4 pound soft dates, pitted
1 tablespoon butter
1/4 cup walnut pieces
1 teaspoon orange juice
For the dough:
2 1/2 cups unbleached, all-purpose flour
1/2 cup cornmeal
1 cup confectioners' sugar
1 cup butter, at room temperature
1 teaspoon *mahlab**
1 teaspoon vanilla
1 teaspoon orange blossom water
1 large egg yolk, beaten with 1 tablespoon of water

Preparation:
Preheat oven to 350°F.

To make the filling, combine dates, butter, walnut pieces, and orange juice in a food processor. Pulse until a thick paste forms. Remove paste and form 24 blueberry-size balls. Set aside on a plate.

Line 2 baking sheets with parchment paper or silicone pads.

Make dough by combining flour, cornmeal, confectioners' sugar, butter, *mahlab*, vanilla, and orange blossom water in a large bowl. Mix until well combined and form a dough ball with your hands.

---

* See "Where to Buy Guide" for purchasing information.

Divide dough into 24 golf-ball-size pieces. Make a hole in the center of each and insert a piece of the date paste. Cover with dough to close the hole and roll back into a ball.

Place cookies 1 inch apart on cookie sheets. Dip a fork in water and use it to slightly flatten the tops of the cookies. Brush the egg yolk mixture on the top of each cookie to coat.

Bake cookies for 15 to 20 minutes, or until lightly golden. Remove from oven and cool in cookie sheets.

Makes 2 dozen.

Tip: Make dough and filling a day in advance, roll both into balls, and refrigerate until ready to assemble and bake.

Entertaining Timeline

One week before the event:
Invite guests.

Confirm guest list and adjust ingredients in recipes to reflect number of guests, if necessary.

Make grocery list.

Buy groceries.

Make Date and Walnut Cookies and freeze.

One day before the event:
Make Date and Raisin Drink.

Make Cornish Hens Glazed with Date Molasses and refrigerate.

Set table.

Day of the event:
Remove cookies from freezer to thaw.

Make Basmati Rice with Dates and Apricots.

Make Date, Orange, and Feta Ball Salad.

Reheat Cornish hens.

Pour drink into serving glasses.

CHAPTER 16
Arabian Dessert Party

Many of our best memories occur while enjoying coffee or tea at home with friends. With this dessert menu, you can make those moments even more memorable. Start by decorating your table with a fresh orchid plant. Give each of your guests a fresh orchid flower when they arrive. Serve them *sahlab,* a smooth, milky drink thickened with ground orchid bulbs. Next, serve one or all three of the delicious desserts listed in the menu. Use the occasion as an opportunity to set out your favorite dishes. The large dessert buffet tables I saw at the palaces in Saudi Arabia inspired these decadent desserts.

Menu
Drink:
> Sweet Orchid Drink (*Sahlab*)
> Arabic Cardamom Coffee (see page 101)
> Black Tea (see page 46)

Desserts:
> Pistachio *K'nafeh* (*Ballouriah*)
> Baba Au Rose (*Baba bil Ward*)
> Fig and Cream Filled Tartlets (*Hellawat bil Teen*
> > *w'Ishta*)

Favor:
> Orchids

Sweet Orchid Drink (Sahlab)

Sahlab (sometimes spelled *sahleb* or *sahlep*) is a smooth, creamy drink that is satisfying enough to take the place of dessert. It's made from the starch found in ground orchid bulbs. Instant *sahlab* mixes are sold in Middle Eastern markets and by ethnic grocers online. Some recommend using cornstarch instead of *sahlab,* but I do not. The unique orchid flavor is what makes this drink so special. Try it on a chilly night instead of hot chocolate; it'll be your new favorite.

Ingredients:

4 cups whole milk
1 packet or 1/4 cup instant *sahlab* powder
1 teaspoon rose water
4 teaspoons unsalted ground nuts (almonds, pistachios, ha-
    zelnuts, or your favorite)
1 teaspoon grated coconut
4 dashes of cinnamon

Preparation:

In a medium saucepan, bring milk to a boil over medium
    heat. Add *sahlab* powder, stir with a wooden spoon, and
    reduce heat to low. Add rose water and continue stir-
    ring. Cook for 2 minutes and remove from heat. Pour
    into 4 clear, heat-proof glasses. Top each with 1 tea-
    spoon nuts and 1/4 teaspoon grated coconut. Sprinkle
    a dash of cinnamon on top of each glass. Serve hot.
Serves 4.

*Tip: If you rinse your saucepan with cold water (and don't
dry it) before you scald the milk in the pot, the saucepan will
not get scorched on the bottom.*

Pistachio K'nafeh (Ballouriah)

Pistachios are native to Western Asia. They were eaten in
Turkey, Afghanistan, and Iran 7,000 years ago. A resin from the
pistachio tree is used to produce mastic, another ingredient in
Middle and Near Eastern cuisines.

This is a unique and delightful *k'nafeh* recipe. Fortunately,
it's easy to prepare. The pistachios used in this recipe can be
replaced with walnuts or almonds, if preferred. *K'nafeh* can be
stored in the refrigerator for up to 3 days, but it is best eaten the
day it is prepared. Keep in mind that this dessert needs to be
weighted down in the refrigerator for at least one hour.

Ingredients:

For the syrup:
1 1/2 cups sugar
2 large strips of orange peel

Juice of 1 small orange
For the filling:
2 cups pistachios
2 tablespoons sugar
1 teaspoon orange blossom water
For the k'nafeh:
4 sticks unsalted butter, melted
1 (1-pound) package *kataifi*,* thawed

Preparation:

To make the syrup, combine sugar, 1 cup water, zest, and
   orange juice in a medium saucepan. Bring to a boil over
   medium heat, stirring with a wooden spoon until sugar
   is dissolved. Stop stirring, reduce heat to low, and let
   simmer approximately 10 to 15 minutes, until syrup
   thickens. Remove from heat and cool. Remove zest from
   syrup.

Preheat oven to 350°F.

To make the filling, combine pistachios, sugar, and orange
   blossom water in a food processor. Pulse until mixture
   is coarsely ground.

To assemble the *k'nafeh*, place melted butter in a large, deep
   bowl. Holding the *kataifi* strands over the butter, pull
   them apart, and toss them with the butter. Use your
   fingers to combine and continue breaking the strands
   up until they are 1 to 2 inches each. Press half of strands
   into the bottom of a 9x13-inch baking pan. Spread pistachio filling evenly over the top. Press the remaining
   kataifi strands over the filling to cover. Cover the surface of the *k'nafeh* with aluminum foil.

Place 2 (5-pound) weights (bags of sugar or cans work fine)
   on top of the *k'nafeh*. Refrigerate 1 hour or up to overnight. Take weights off and remove foil from *k'nafeh*.

With a sharp, long, serrated knife, carefully make 30
   squares inside the pan (be careful not to cut through

---

* Sold as "shredded phyllo strands." See "Where to Buy Guide" for
purchasing information.

the bottom layer of *kataifi*). Place in the oven and bake for 1 hour and 20 minutes, rotating pan every 20 minutes to ensure even baking. *K'nafeh* is finished when it is golden in color.

Carefully pour syrup over *k'nafeh* after removing it from oven. Let cool completely and use a spatula to serve. *Serves 10.*

Tip: You can make the syrup and filling up to a month ahead of time. They can be stored in airtight containers in the refrigerator. Assemble and weigh the k'nafeh the night before serving it. Then, on the day of serving, you'll need only to cut it, bake it, and pour the syrup on top.

Baba Au Rose (*Baba bil Ward*)

Baba Au Rose is a spin-off of the classic Baba Au Rhum, which was invented in the seventeenth century by Polish King Stanislas Leszczynski, father-in-law of Louis XV of France. The king soaked his stale kugelhopf in rum and named the creation after Ali Baba, a main character in his favorite *1,001 Arabian Nights* story. In this version, I've replaced the rum with a simple syrup and an apricot-rose water glaze. Given the popularity and extensive use of rose water in the Arabian Peninsula, I believe this preparation is more appropriate.

Ingredients:

For the syrup:
1 1/2 cups sugar
2 large strips of orange peel
Juice of 1 small orange

For the Baba:
Canola oil cooking spray
1/2 cup whole milk
1 package active dry yeast
1/3 cup plus 2 tablespoons sugar, divided
2 large eggs, at room temperature
1 2/3 cups unbleached, all-purpose flour
1/2 teaspoon salt
4 tablespoons unsalted butter, at room temperature

3/4 cup apricot preserves
1 tablespoon rose water
Whipped cream, for garnish
Fresh strawberries, for garnish

Preparation:

To make the syrup, combine sugar, 1 cup water, peel, and orange juice in a medium saucepan. Bring to a boil over medium heat, stirring with a wooden spoon until sugar is dissolved. Stop stirring, reduce heat to low, and let simmer approximately 10 to 15 minutes, until syrup thickens. Remove from heat and set aside to cool. Remove zest from syrup.

Grease Baba molds with cooking spray. Be sure to cover all parts of the mold.

In a small saucepan over medium heat, heat the milk to 115°F. Pour warm milk into the bowl of an electric mixer fitted with a paddle attachment. Add the yeast and 2 tablespoons of sugar to the milk and let rest for 15 minutes. Add the eggs with the mixer running on low speed, and mix to combine well. Slowly add the flour, the remaining 1/3 cup sugar, salt, and butter, beating on low speed. Mix well and beat for 5 minutes on medium speed. Remove bowl from mixer and cover it with plastic wrap and a clean kitchen towel. Set in a draft-free location for 1 hour to let batter rise.

Punch down the dough, cover, and let rise for another 2 hours. At this point, the mixture should be very bubbly and almost reach the top of the bowl.

Preheat oven to 375°F.

Spoon 2 to 2 1/2 tablespoons of dough into each Baba mold. Tap the bottoms of the molds on the counter to release air bubbles. Place the molds on a cookie sheet and bake for 10 to 15 minutes, until they are light golden. Remove from the oven. Cool for 10 minutes.

In the meantime, mix apricot preserves, 1 tablespoon of water, and rose water together in a small saucepan over low heat until mixture reaches a liquid consistency. Remove from heat and set aside.

Turn the Baba molds over and tap on the bottoms to release the Babas. Place them in a shallow bowl and drizzle syrup over each one. Let sit for 10 minutes to absorb the syrup.

Remove Babas one at a time and brush apricot glaze over each one. Place on a serving platter. Garnish with whipped cream and fresh strawberries. Serve warm or at room temperature.

Serves 4 to 6.

Tip: Babas are prepared in special molds that look like deep oval-shaped metal tins. They can be purchased at most kitchen and baking supply stores.

Fig and Cream Filled Tartlets (Hellawat bil Teen w'Ishta)

The popular Arabian *ishta* cream is the star of this spectacular dessert. Since *ishta* can be purchased ready-made all over the Arab world, many people don't bother to prepare it themselves. Luckily, it's simple to make and consists of easy-to-find ingredients. Once you learn how easy it is, you'll find a variety of applications for it. Many people eat the cream with honey and bread or pastries for breakfast. Remember: do not stir the *ishta* cream with a metal spoon or whisk for a long period of time or the cream will separate.

Ingredients:
Canola oil cooking spray
For the dough:
3 cups unbleached, all-purpose flour
1 cup unsalted butter, at room temperature
3/4 cup confectioners' sugar
1 teaspoon vanilla
1 large egg yolk
1/2 cup fig jam
For the istha *cream:*
2 cups heavy whipping cream
4 tablespoons cornstarch, diluted in 1/4 cup water
1/4 cup sugar

1 teaspoon orange blossom water
1 teaspoon rose water
For the topping:
3 teaspoons orange blossom honey
1/4 cup shelled pistachios, coarsely chopped

Preparation:

Grease a 12-hole muffin pan with cooking spray.

Combine flour and butter in a large bowl. Mix to combine well. Add sugar, vanilla, and egg yolk. Mix well to form a dough. Form dough into a ball and wrap it in plastic wrap or aluminum foil. Refrigerate for 30 minutes.

Remove dough from refrigerator and form it into 12 balls of equal size. Place 1 ball in each hole of the muffin tin and press down with fingers to line muffin hole completely. Repeat until each hole is covered with dough. Prick the bottoms and sides of each piece of dough with a fork in several places. Place muffin tin in refrigerator for 1 hour. (This can be done a day in advance.)

In the meantime, make the filling: Heat cream to 115°F in a medium saucepan over medium heat. Turn heat down to low before cream boils and stir in cornstarch mixture. Increase heat to medium and whisk mixture to prevent lumps from forming. Whisk in sugar and mix well. Bring to a boil, stirring with a wooden spoon vigorously, and allow to boil for 2 minutes. Reduce heat to low, and stir slowly until a thick custard forms. Cream is done cooking when it is reduced to half of its original volume and you are able to see a "path" at the bottom of the custard as you stir it. Remove cream from heat and set aside. Stir in orange blossom water and rose water with a wooden spoon. Cool. (This can be done a day in advance.)

Preheat oven to 350°F.

After the tartlets have been chilled for an hour, bake them for 10 minutes, or until they turn lightly golden. Remove from oven and spoon a teaspoon of fig jam into the center of each one. Cool in muffin pan.

When cool, turn pan out onto a surface and tap the bottoms

of each tartlet with a metal spoon to release. Turn the tartlets over, fill each with a few tablespoons of cream, and drizzle honey over each one. Garnish with a few pistachio pieces.

Serves 12.

Tip: You can make the tartlets ahead of time and freeze them. On the day you need them, defrost and fill them. It is best to fill them on the day you serve them.

Entertaining Timeline

One week before party:
Invite guests.
Confirm guest list and adjust quantities in recipes accordingly, if necessary.
Make grocery list.
Mail order or buy special ingredients, if necessary.
Buy groceries.

One day before the party:
Make Pistachio *K'nafeh*.
Make Fig and Cream Filled Tartlets, but do not fill.
Set table.

Day of the party:
Make Baba Au Rose.
Fill Fig and Cream Filled Tartlets.
Make *Sahlab*.
Brew coffee and tea as guests arrive.

Glossary

Allspice   Frequently used spice that can be purchased ground or whole, as berries, and ground as needed.

Anise seeds   Seeds used since antiquity in Egypt in beverages, sweets, and savory stews. It is also used as a natural diuretic, digestion aid, breath freshener, cough suppressant, and cholesterol lowerer.

Arabic coffee   A lightly roasted, golden-hued coffee, usually infused with cardamom.

Baharat   Arabic name given to various spice mixes throughout the Arab world. Each country has its own basic *baharat* for fish, poultry, and meat. Homemade mixes vary according to prices, availability, and personal preference.

Basmati rice   Fragrant Indian rice with long, slender grains grown at the base of the Himalayas. Referred to as the "Prince of Rice" because of its taste.

Bizaar   Omani spice mixture used in many savory recipes.

Caraway   Seeds used as a spice or fresh leaves used as an herb. Trays are kept underneath growing caraway plants to catch falling seeds.

Cardamom   A spice native to India and considered to be India's favorite spice. The green variety is extremely important in Arabian cuisine and is featured in everything from drinks to savory dishes to sweet desserts. Cardamom can be bought whole in its pods, which need to be opened to remove its seeds, and ground.

Chai Hot tea drink native to Southeastern Asia that is steeped in various spices.

Chapati Traditional unleavened bread of India that is made with leavening and clarified butter in Pakistan and the Arabian Peninsula. Traditionally baked in a clay oven.

Chili powder Spice made from dried hot chilies. The degree of hotness of chili powders varies greatly. Choose one that suits your own taste.

Cilantro An herb usually added to a dish at the end of a meal to maintain its flavor or used in salads. Dried, ground cilantro is called coriander.

Cinnamon A spice available in sticks or ground. The cinnamon sold in the Arabian Peninsula is pure, meaning it contains no cassia, unlike that sold in the United States. It is milder in flavor and is used in both sweet and savory recipes. Cinnamon is believed to regulate blood sugar levels.

Clarified butter Clarified butter is now readily available in the United States. It is sold under the name ghee and is often found among Indian grocery items. In the Arabian Peninsula, it is called *samn* and is available in varieties made from goat, cow, sheep, and buffalo milk. There are also vegetable varieties. To clarify butter at home, melt butter and skim the white solids off the top with a spoon.

Cloves The unopened buds of an evergreen tree native

to the East Indies and eastern Africa. They are used whole and ground in marinades, preserves, stocks, stews, and sweets. Clove oil is sold as an antiseptic and opened clove buds make beautiful carnation-like fragrant flowers.

Coriander A spice made from dried cilantro seeds. It imparts a sweet and spicy flavor to savory dishes and is also used to stimulate digestion and promote relaxation.

Couscous Tiny, round Moroccan-style pasta made of semolina and coarsely ground durum wheat flour. Its name originates from the Berber word *k'seksu*. Traditionally hand-rolled, manufactured couscous is available in instant varieties in supermarkets. Israeli couscous consists of larger, pearl-like pasta beads.

Cracked wheat Wheat berries used in many savory dishes in the Arabian Peninsula.

Cumin A spice found in numerous savory recipes from Asia, the Middle East, Africa, and Latin America. It has a pungent flavor and is known to aid digestion, dispel gas, and have laxative properties. Because of its strong aroma, it should be stored in an airtight glass jar away from other spices and foods.

Date molasses A syrup extracted from dried dates, one of the Arabian Peninsula's most important agricultural crops.

Dill An herb native to the Mediterranean region that is mainly used fresh, not dried, in the Arabian Peninsula. Dill is rich in minerals.

Dried lemons Dried fruit used primarily in Persian and Arabian

(Limoon Aghmani)	cuisines to impart a tart flavor to soups and stews. Usually made from thin-skinned *daq* lemons.
Dried limes *(Lumi)*	Dried fruit used primarily in Persian and Arabian cuisines. They are often ground and added to various spice mixes or used in soups and stews.
Dried rosebuds	The dried buds of roses, which can be added to teas and stocks to enhance their flavors.
Eid	The Arabic word for holiday, used by Muslims worldwide.
Eid al Adha	A four-day Muslim holiday celebrated after the annual pilgrimage to Mecca. It is also known as the "*Eid Kabeer*," or the "Big Holiday." In English, it is often referred to as "the Feast of the Sacrifice" because Muslims sacrifice lambs in commemoration of Abraham, who was ordered to sacrifice a lamb in place of his beloved son. This holiday is celebrated with lamb dishes, visits with relatives, alms giving, and gifts.
Eid al Fitr	A three-day Muslim holiday marking the end of the month of Ramadan and celebrated with various foods, visits with relatives, alms giving, and gifts.
Fatayer	Savory bread pies of Lebanese origin, often stuffed with cheese, meat, or spinach. They have become a popular Arabian street food.
Fattoush	A tangy Lebanese salad that combines fried pita bread with fresh vegetables, topped with a pomegranate dressing.

Fennel seeds   The seeds of the fennel plant that add a sweet taste to savory dishes. Often eaten roasted or as a tea to assist digestion and freshen breath.

Fenugreek (*hilba*) Seeds from a plant native to Egypt, India, and various countries in the Arabian Peninsula. They are believed to cure respiratory problems and indigestion. Islamic healer's once claimed, "If people knew the benefits of fenugreek, they would pay for its weight in gold." It is a common addition to teas, spice mixes, and relishes.

Flat Leaf Parsley An herb added to many salads and appetizers or used as a garnish. Parsley contains vitamins A, B, C, iron, and calcium. It is also a natural breath freshener and aids digestion.

Garam masala   The most common Indian spice mix, which has become popular in the Arabian Peninsula. It typically consists of clove, cardamom, cumin, peppercorns, and cinnamon, although many variations exist.

Ghorayeba   A cardamom-infused shortbread cookie from Saudi Arabia.

Ginger   A spice that lends a warm touch to soups, spice mixes, stews, and beverages. Early Arabian spice traders brought ginger back from India. In India, ginger is thought to be capable of burning up toxins. It is used to relieve muscle inflammation, motion sickness, morning sickness, and indigestion.

Hadith   The recorded words, actions, and sanctions of the Prophet Muhammad. The *hadith* and the *Qur'an* are used by Sunni Muslims to interpret Islam.

Hajj

The pilgrimage to Mecca, Saudi Arabia, that is required of observant Muslims. The *hajj* may take place only one time per year and this date is based on the lunar-based Islamic calendar. During the *hajj,* Muslims worship God by performing a series of rituals based on traditions started by the Prophet Abraham and the Prophet Muhammad.

Halal

Permissible or lawful. The term denotes those things that observant Muslims may partake in according to the mandates of Islam. For culinary purposes, the word *halal* is used to describe meat upon which the name of God has been pronounced before it is killed. *Halal* regulations mandate that the animal be killed in a manner that does not prolong trauma or suffering and that its blood be drained before it is consumed. It is only considered *halal* to kill animals for the purpose of consumption. Sport hunting is not permissible in Islam.

Haram

Unlawful, the opposite of *halal. Haram* foods in Islam are the flesh, blood, and skin of swine, any meat upon which God's name has not been pronounced, and alcohol.

Henna

Flowers that grow on large trees in the Arabian Peninsula and also the paste made from dried henna flowers mixed with water. The paste is placed into a plastic bag or special applicator and piped onto the hands. Henna tattoos are a popular process of female beautification across the Arabian Peninsula. Many henna artists give tattoos freehand whereas novices use stencils to trace the designs on the body. Henna is believed to have special curative powers.

Hijazi

The western region of Saudi Arabia that borders

the Red Sea. Mecca, Medina, Al-Ta'if, and Jeddah are located in this region.

Hommus   Chickpeas.

Iftar   The meal eaten after sundown during Ramadan.

Imam   Islamic leader of formal (congregational) prayers.

Istakbal   Social gatherings, ranging from very casual to formal, held to help friends keep abreast of one another's lives.

Isthta   Cooked cream that is thickened to a pudding-like consistency. Eaten at breakfast and with sweets, it is similar to clotted cream.

Jeddah   Port city located on the Red Sea in Saudi Arabia.

Kabsah   One of the most popular dishes is Saudi Arabian cuisine, consisting of rice, and meat, seafood, or poultry simmered in aromatics.

Kataifi   Sold as "shredded phyllo strands" but actually made by piping phyllo batter into hot oil with a thin-tipped funnel to make angel-hair-width strands. The strands are sold dried. Traditionally used in making sweets, the strands are reconstituted in butter and layered with nut or fruit fillings.

Khaliji   Saudi Arabia's eastern border with the Arabian Sea and, in Arabic countries in North Africa, the manner of countries of the Arabian Peninsula collectively. Arabian cuisine and music are referred to as *khaliji* by outsiders.

K'nafeh	A classic Middle Eastern dessert made by layering *kataifi* strands with nuts or fruit, baking them, and covering them with a sweet syrup.
Kofta	Kabobs made with ground meat.
Labna	Cheese made from cow's, goat's, or sheep's milk yogurt. Sometimes sold as *labne* or *lebni*.
Lavash	A Middle Eastern flat bread perfect for rolling sandwiches.
Machbous	A Kuwaiti dish consisting of mutton, fish, or chicken cooked with fragrant rice. It's similar to Saudi Arabian *kabsah* and Indian *biryani*.
Mahallabeya	A popular milk pudding traditionally thickened with rice flour.
Mahlab	Ground cherry kernels used as a flavoring in sweets.
Makhtoum	A dish made from very tender meat or poultry that has been marinated and cooked in yogurt.
Ma'moul	Arabian cookies made in special wooden molds. They may be stuffed with dates, nuts, or fruit.
Mecca	Spelled Makkah in Saudi Arabia. The ancient city in Saudi Arabia that is considered the birthplace of Islam. Each year Muslims from around the globe participate in a pilgrimage to the Great Mosque in Mecca whose original structure was built by the Prophet Abraham. Traveling to Mecca to complete the pilgrimage is one of the five pillars of Islam. All Muslims must face in the direction of Mecca when they pray.

Medina	A city in eastern Saudi Arabia where the Prophet Muhammad lived after he emigrated from Mecca in 622. It is famous for his namesake mosque, "The Prophet's Mosque," as well as many other historically significant Islamic sights.
Mina	An ancient town near Mecca, Saudi Arabia, where pilgrims spend certain nights during *hajj* to perform religious rituals.
Mint	Herb that may be used fresh or in a dried, ground form. Mint is a traditional accompaniment to tea and sugar. It is also a main component of salads and is used in spice mixes. Mint is known to freshen the breath and calm upset stomachs.
Namoura	A mildly sweet dessert cake made with semolina flour.
Nigella seeds (Habit al Baraka)	Believed to be a cure for everything other than death, black nigella seeds are often added to Arabian breads and pickling mixtures. Medicinal oil is also extracted from them.
Nutmeg	A spice used extensively in Arabian spice mixes. Arabians buy whole pods of nutmeg and grate them just before using. Nutmeg should be stored in a glass container to preserve freshness.
Orange blossom water	Water made from orange blossom oils that is used as a flavoring for syrups and sweets.
Paprika	A spice made, in the Arabian Peninsula, from dried, crushed, sweet red peppers, not the smoked variety. Store paprika and other red colored spices in the refrigerator.

Poppy seeds   Black seeds used as a garnish for both savory and sweet dishes. Their gritty texture enhances the moistness of baked goods.

Qur'an   The Muslim holy book that was revealed to the Prophet Muhammad in Mecca, Saudi Arabia, during the seventh century.

Ramadan   The ninth lunar month of the Islamic calendar. Muslims believe that Ramadan is the month in which the *Torah*, *Bible*, and *Qur'an* were all revealed. Fasting from sunup to sundown during this month is the fourth pillar of Islam and is meant to promote self-discipline and piety.

Rice flour   Flour made from ground rice often used as a thickening agent.

Rose water   Water made from the distillation of rose oil. Used to enhance the flavor of drinks, syrups, and sweets.

Saffron   The world's most expensive spice. It is cultivated from the stigmas of the crocus flower in fall. Its English name is derived from the plural form of the feminine form of the Arabic word for yellow, *saffra*. Saffron provides a bright yellow pigment and unique flavor to drinks, savories, and sweets. Medicinally, saffron is said to increase energy, suppress coughs, have diuretic properties, rejuvenate the heart, and ease labor pains.

Sahlab   A powder made from ground orchid bulbs. A drink made by mixing the powder with hot milk goes by the same name.

Sambusak   Savory pastries usually filled with ground meat that are popular in Saudi Arabia.

Sesame seeds   Seeds produced by the attractive flowers of the tropical sesame plant as they dry up. The plants yield approximately a tablespoon of seeds per pod. The seeds contain protein, phosphorus, niacin, sulfur, and carbohydrates and are used whole and to make culinary oils and pastes.

Semolina   Flour made with hard wheat. It is most frequently used in the Arabian Peninsula in recipes for sweets and breads.

Shish barak   Meat-filled dumplings made in Saudi Arabia and Lebanon. Many variations exist in other cultures and include Italian tortelloni and Armenian and Turkish *manti*.

Sohoor   The pre-dawn breakfast meal eaten during the month of Ramadan.

Sumac   A spice made by grinding the seeds of the sumac plant, a member of the cashew family. It has a beautiful red color and gives a tangy taste to chicken, eggs, spice mixes, rice, and dips.

Tabbouli   A salad of Lebanese origin that consists of bulgur wheat with cucumbers, onions, and tomatoes.

Tahini   A sesame seed paste, called *tahina* in Arabic.

Tajine   A clay pot used to slowly cook stews in the Middle East. In Morocco, the pot is distinguished by its conical shaped lid. All recipes made with a *tajine* have the word in their title.

Tamarind   The dried, dark brown pod of the tamarind plant. The English word "tamarind" comes from the Arabic words *tamr hindi*, meaning Indian date. The pod needs to be soaked in water before it can be used. Tamarind paste and syrup are used extensively in the Indian subcontinent, the Middle East, Africa, the Caribbean, and Latin America.

Turmeric A bright yellow spice with a bitter flavor. It is used as a stain in various Indian festivals and has various medicinal properties, including use as sunscreen and insect repellent. Be careful not to stain your hands or clothes when using it.

Wild thyme A variety of thyme native to the Middle East. It can be used in breads, meat, poultry, soups, and stews. It is known in Arabic as *zataar*. An Arabian spice mix that includes wild thyme is referred to as *zataar* in Arabic as well.

Where to Buy Guide

Adriana's Caravan

www.adrianascaravan.com

Spices, including *baharat*, dried lemon, dried rosebuds, fenugreek, *garam masala*, *mahlab*, nigella seeds, saffron, sumac, and *zataar*. Also, bulgur, couscous, date molasses, fava beans, orange blossom water, pomegranate molasses, rose water, spice grinders, and tahini.

Aphrodite Greek and Middle Eastern Imports

5886 Leesburg Pike
Falls Church, VA 22041
(703) 931-5055

Wide assortment of cheeses, incense, and incense burners. Bulgur, clarified butter, couscous, cracked wheat, date molasses, dates, grape leaves, hulled grain, *kataifi*, *labna*, *mahlab*, *ma'moul* molds, nigella seeds, rose water, orange blossom water, phyllo, pomegranate molasses, rice flour, saffron, *sahlab*, semolina, sumac, tahini, tamarind paste, and *zataar*.

Arabian Bazaar

www.arabianbazaar.com

Wood incense (called *oudh*), incense burners, and fragrances.

The Brainy Bean

(866) 473-2055
www.thebrainybean.com

Yemeni coffee, spices, flavored syrups, and Ceylon tea.

Kalustyan's

123 Lexington Avenue
New York, NY 10016
(212) 685-3451

www.kalustyans.com

Arabic coffee (plain or with cardamom), Arabic coffee cups, Arabic coffee pots, *baharat*, bulgur, Ceylon tea, clarified butter, coconut milk, couscous, date molasses, dates, dried lemons, dried limes, dried rose petals, fava beans, fenugreek, frankincense, *garam masala*, grape leaves, grenadine, hulled grain (sold as *frik*), incense (sold as *bakhour*), lavash and pita bread, *mahlab*, myrrh, nigella seeds, orange blossom water, rice flour, rose water, tahini, saffron, sesame seeds, sumac, and *zataar*.

Nile Style
(301) 910-8560
www.nilestylefragrances.com

Pure, undiluted fragrance essences, including Arabian Lily of the Valley, Lotus Flower, Papyrus, Secret of the Desert, and Summer Jasmine.

Tattoo Me
(310) 575-1441
www.tattoo-me.com

Henna paste, applicators, stencils, and accessories.

Bibliography

Al-Akili, Muhammad. *Natural Healing with the Medicine of the Prophet: From the Book of the Provisions of the Hereafter.* Philadelphia: Pearl Publishing House, 1993.

Ali, Abdullah Yusuf, trans. *The Holy Qur'an.* New Delhi: Kitab Bhavan, 1996.

Bridgewater Book Company, Ltd. *The Best Ever Indian Cookbook.* Bath, UK: Parragon Publishing, 2003.

Embassy of the Kingdom of Bahrain. *Gateway to the Gulf.* Washington, DC: Embassy of the Kingdom of Bahrain, Fall 2004.

Hattstein, Markus, and Delius, Peter. *Islam: Art and Architecture.* Germany: Konemann, 2004.

Hill, Margaret. *It's Pomegranate Season.* (Chemistry.Org: The Website of the American Chemical Society), December 19, 2005.

Hyams, Gina. *Incense: Rituals, Mystery, Lore.* San Francisco: Chronicle Books, 2004.

Ibrahim, Ezzedin, and Johnson-Davies, Denys, trans. *An-Nawawi's Forty Hadith.*

Kaufman, Sheilah. *Sephardic Israeli Cuisine: A Mediterranean Mosaic.* New York: Hippocrene Books, 2002.

Lebling, Robert W., and Pepperdine, Donna. "Natural Remedies of Arabia." *Saudi Aramco World,* September–October 2006, 17–18.

Medical Studies/Trials. *Pomegranate Juice Helps Keep Fatty Deposits from Collecting on Artery Walls.* (News-Medical.net), March 22, 2005.

Sakr, Ahmed Hussein. *Feast, Festivities & Holidays.* Lombard, IL: Foundation for Islamic Knowledge, 1999.

Sultanate of Oman Ministry of Tourism. *Sultanate of Oman.* Muscat, Oman: International Printing Press, n.d.

Index

About the Author

Amy Riolo is an internationally recognized culinary expert, cookbook author, food historian, food writer, and cooking instructor who lives in the Washington, D.C., area. She has spent the past decade researching and creating Middle Eastern recipes for and teaching the recipes to American audiences. The opportunity to travel extensively throughout the region has increased Amy's passion for authentic Middle Eastern cuisine. While writing *Arabian Delights*, Amy received culinary inspiration from the palaces, homes, street vendors, restaurants, cafes, and markets she visited in Saudi Arabia.

Amy is a member of the International Association of Culinary Professionals, Les Dames d'Escoffier, the Culinary Historians of Washington, Slow Food DC, Welcome to Washington International (for which she is a member of the Gourmet Committee), the Baltimore-Luxor-Alexandria Sister City Committee (for which she is the Egyptian culture and cuisine online editor), and the Cornell Club of DC. Amy maintains a home in Egypt and travels to the region as often as possible to keep abreast of culinary trends.

Artist, illustrationist, and teacher **Liana Mari** was born in Copparo Ferrara, Italy. She graduated from art school in Rome, Italy, where she majored in painting, trompe l'oeil, and decorative arts. Although her favorite painters are Dechirico and Magritte, Liana loves all forms of artistic expression that are pleasing to both her eyes and her heart. Today Liana lives in Rome with her husband and son. She enjoys foreign travel immensely and continues to receive creative inspiration through experiencing the arts of daily living in various cultures.